DO-IT-YOURSELF
TAILORED
SLIPCOVERS

DO-IT-YOURSELF
TAILORED
SLIPCOVERS

Sophia Sevo

4880 Lower Valley Road, Atglen, Pennsylvania 19310

Schiffer Books are available at special discounts for bulk
purchases for sales promotions or premiums. Special edi-
tions, including personalized covers, corporate imprints,
and excerpts can be created in large quantities for special
needs. For more information contact the publisher:

Published by Schiffer Publishing Ltd.
4880 Lower Valley Road
Atglen, PA 19310
Phone: (610) 593-1777; Fax: (610) 593-2002
E-mail: Info@schifferbooks.com

For the largest selection of fine reference books on this and
related subjects, please visit our web site at:
www.schifferbooks.com
We are always looking for people to write books on new
and related subjects. If you have an idea for a book please
contact us at the above address.

This book may be purchased from the publisher.
Include $5.00 for shipping.
Please try your bookstore first.
You may write for a free catalog.

In Europe, Schiffer books are distributed by
Bushwood Books
6 Marksbury Ave.
Kew Gardens
Surrey TW9 4JF England
Phone: 44 (0) 20 8392-8585; Fax: 44 (0) 20 8392-9876
E-mail: info@bushwoodbooks.co.uk
Website: www.bushwoodbooks.co.uk
Free postage in the U.K., Europe; air mail at cost.

Acknowledgments

I would like to thank Melissa Norbeck at Waverly for her outstanding support throughout this project. Thanks to Waverly for graciously supplying the fabric for the following chapters: chapter three, outdoor bench; chapter five, Bergere chair; chapter six, wingback chair; chapter seven; club chair; chapter eight, parsons chair; chapter nine, contemporary chair. Waverly also supplied the cleaning codes and fabric care instructions in chapter one.

I would also like to thank past Waverly alumni Lucille Grippo and Glenda Guerri. Thanks to Sherry and Sarah at the FSCO showroom in Troy, MI for your wonderful help in the showroom.

Special thanks to Bob Lesniak at Woeller for your wonderful service over the years. Thanks to Jon Woeller for your support and help during this project. Woeller fabrics are featured in the following chapters: chapter one, introduction; chapter two, sofa; chapter four, headboard.

Thanks to Karen Hall at the Windsor Star for your support over the years.

A special thanks to Detroit and Windsor customs, for accommodating me when documents that accompanied equipment and materials were not correctly prepared.

A great, big thank you to all of my family and friends who have helped out over the years; Mom and Dad, my brothers Alex and Sasha and fiancée Karrie, my sister Sandy, my uncles Mile and George, my aunt Stephanie, Ujak and Ujna, my cousins Dana and Draga, and my friends and neighbors Aziz B. and Mario M.

Thanks to Ed Sears and Bob Hubbard for accommodating a last minute photo request, it is greatly appreciated.

Special thanks to Charlie Brown for your help and for collaborating on the upcoming ottoman line. You will make this dream a success.

Dedication

It is my hope that I have written a book which will enable the experienced and those who possess only will and determination.

I toast, to all of the treasures born of good working hands.

Inside this Book

Chapter One
An Introduction to Slipcovers

A tailored slipcover is a wonderful way to beautify your home, because it gives you the freedom to reinvent your decor and the flexibility to move your furniture from room to room. Fitting a tailored slipcover takes time, patience, and precision. Changes and adjustments are guaranteed throughout the learning process, and thereafter! But with experience, you will be the proud craftsman—or craftswoman—of coveted tailored slipcovers.

Draping a Slipcover

I do not recommend that a slipcover is draped first in muslin for use as a pattern to cut another fabric. I always drape my slipcovers in the final fabric, and in doing so, create the best slipcover for that fabric in a specific application. Every textile has its own unique properties that need to be considered, accommodated, and tolerated. Some fabrics may not press well, or some may dimple over concave curves. If the aesthetic qualities of a textile take precedence over performance, the nature of the fabric will have to be tolerated. This is true for all textiles, regardless of the application. Pattern size, fabric direction, and finish are all dictated by the inherent properties of a textile. The sofa in chapter two is a perfect example. The original arm front of this upholstered sofa was cut on the straight grain. When the arm front was reupholstered in Woellers' Another Suede, it had to be cut on the bias.

For slipcovers, some textiles will benefit from the addition of a knit backing on the reverse side. Fabrics such as microsuede because they are prone to static build-up, and lower weight fabrics such as silk will benefit from the added strength. If you purchase your fabric through an upholstery shop or designer, adding knit backing is a service that can be provided through your fabric supplier.

Woeller fabrics available with knit backing; shown are Suedetex II in Chambray and Suedetex 1000 in Royal Purple.

Woeller fabrics available with knit backing; shown, Simply Silk in Grassgreen and Rose Petal.

In draping, if you are working with furniture that is upholstered in a print, do not use the upholstery as a guide to center the pattern of your slipcover. Always measure the width of the frame, locate the center points, and insert pins into the upholstery. When draping a pattern that requires centering, feel for the pins and place the center of the blocks over them.

For details on draping with patterns, refer to the Bergere chair slipcover found in chapter five.

Terminology

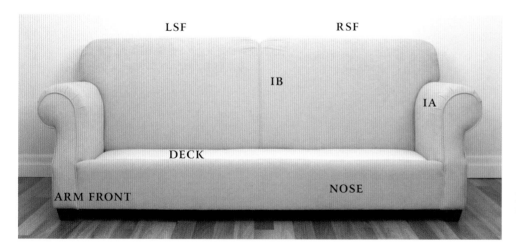

Illustrating furniture terminology.

LSF	Left side facing	SA	Seam allowance
RSF	Right side facing	LAF	Left arm facing
NOSE	Nose	RAF	Right arm facing
DECK	Deck	ARM FRONT	Arm front
IA	Inside arm	IW	Inside wing
IB	Inside Back	OW	Outside wing
OB	Outside back	RSD	Right side down
OA	Outside arm	RSU	Right side up

Yardage and Textiles

The typical width for upholstery fabric is 54"; the fabrics are cut in two directions: "regular," or "railroaded." "Regular" refers to the common way that the majority of fabrics are cut, including garment textiles, where the straight grain runs parallel to the selvage. The "railroaded" direction seen in upholstery fabrics is less common in garment curtting. In this layout, the straight grain is perpendicular to the selvage. Generally, less yardage is required when a project is cut in the railroaded direction.

Yardage is always calculated *after* a fabric has been chosen. Fabric width, cutting direction, and knowing if the fabric is a match or can be cut as a solid is required information for an accurate estimate.

A soft tape is used to measure the length and width of each component in a slipcover. The measurements, called blocks, are used to calculate yardage and to drape each corresponding component. While I accurately measure the width of the IB and IA to include tucking fabric, I always allocate 5" for the tucking length. For all IB and IA blocks measuring the length will stop at the deck, plus 5".

During fitting, changes to the tucking length will be made according to the available depth, and any adjustment will be made during the fitting. The length of tucking fabric should always equal the distance into the frame, never more. When pushed into the sides of a frame, the tucking fabric should lay flat. Too much tucking fabric will compress foam, shortening the life span of your furniture. Heavier weight fabrics in tight spaces may necessitate even less tucking fabric than the available depth, if the tucking fabric causes foam to compress.

It is, after all, a good fit, and not excessive tucking fabric, that keeps a slipcover in place! The yardage required to create a tailored slipcover is equal to that of upholstery, but unlike upholstery, all raw edges must be overlocked. After draping, each component of a slipcover is overlocked separately. This will ensure that any adjustments during the fitting process are quick and clean. Even with careful handling, some fabrics will fray quickly. Tapestries will be some of the most difficult fabrics to handle and will need to be overlocked immediately.

For details on working with blocks, refer to the wingback slipcover found in chapter six.

Shrinkage

Most upholstery-grade fabrics available through suppliers are not sold as washable. If you plan to wash a slipcover, it is imperative that your fabric is washed before cutting, and that shrinkage is factored into a yardage estimate.

Zippers

The amount and length of zippers needed on a slipcover will depend on the shape of the frame and the style and size of the arm. If the frame is straight, or does not narrow at the base, a zipper may not be necessary to facilitate dressing and removal.

However, a zipper, or two, will make dressing easier when:
- You are working with large frames. Getting the slipcover into position will take less time.
- You are working with heavier weight fabrics. A finished slipcover for a sofa can be quite heavy.
- You are working with fabrics that create static.
- The fabric on the upholstered piece creates resistance against the slipcover fabric.

To calculate shrinkage:

Cut one yard of fabric and launder.

Calculate the percentage of shrinkage. If your fabric is reduced by 2" in a 36" length (one yard), the shrinkage rate is 5.6%.

Therefore, the total estimate will increase by 5.6%.

Take note of any shrinkage across the width of the fabric. When calculating yardage, this will be the new width of your fabric.

Before starting your project, all of your slipcover fabric will need to be laundered. Total shrinkage must be factored for each block so that your fabric can be cut at reasonable lengths according tot he size of your washer. In preparing this estimate, you can lay your blocks out on paper using the one yard length as a reference.

For some fabrics, overlocking the ends to prevent excessive fraying during washing will be necessary. For others you can simply allow some extra length. As well, you may want to take extra precautions with a second washing, as some fabrics can continue to shrink.

For details on working with blocks, refer to the wingback slipcover created in chapter six.

Velcro®

Whenever a slipcover wraps under the frame, I use Velcro® to finish the hem. Soft Velcro® tape is always sewn to the slipcover, so that no damage is incurred to the fabric during washing or dry-cleaning. Rough Velcro® tape is always stapled under the frame. If you are not using a pneumatic stapler to drive staples, the staples may not drive deep into hard wood and the constant pull on Velcro® tape will cause the staples to lift. **IMPORTANT!** Always test and verify that staples are properly embedded into the frame and cannot be pulled out.

To begin, outline the frame with chalk and cut a minimum of 1" and a maximum of 1.5" below the chalk line. On most furniture, the frame width will not exceed 1.5", and so it is not necessary to cut a wider hem that will not have a surface to which it can adhere. Overlock any raw edges and sew a 1" wide Velcro® tape to the cover. When sewing soft tape to the slipcover, do not line the Velcro® with the edge of the fabric, place the tape slightly ahead to cover the overlocked edge. This will help protect the threads from snagging when they come in contact with the rough tape under the frame.

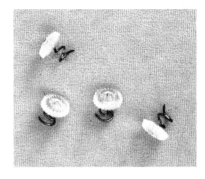

FIG 1.2 Upholstery twist pins are used to secure the front deck of a slipcover.

The Deck

On my slipcovers, I do not cover the deck area of a chair under the seat. With age, springs require repair, which would quickly affect the position of a slipcover by pulling down on the IB and IA. Leaving the deck uncovered guarantees the longest use of a slipcover free from constant adjustment.

Upholstery twist pins are used to hold the front deck in place.

Sewing

Unlike upholstery, all raw edges on a slipcover must be overlocked, and each component should be overlocked separately so that fit adjustments are quick and clean. When sewing, it is sometimes necessary to cut fabric through the overlocked edge. Turning a corner on a seat case is a prime example, and the properties of your fabric will determine whether or not the fabric will need to be cut. **IMPORTANT!** Once any cut is made through an overlocked edge, the corner has to be reinforced to keep the fabric and the overlock thread from unraveling.

Place the cut corner under your sewing machine and using a straight stitch; run through the slash back and forth until all raw edges and overlock threads have been sewn down.

Slipcover Exceptions

Some furniture pieces are not good slipcover candidates. Experience and good judgment will be your guide. One exception is furniture upholstered in leather. The smooth surface of leather will not keep fabric dimensions stable, and this will cause stress on seams and fabric stretching.

I also do not recommend the use of latex-backed fabrics for slipcovers. In time, the latex backing will crumble and disintegrate; when this happens, there is always a chance that damage can occur to the upholstery under the slipcover.

Cleaning Codes

The following are standard definitions of the codes, as applied by fabric houses and furniture manufacturers:

W   Water-based cleaning agents or foam may be used for cleaning. Professional cleaning is recommended.

S   Only mild, pure, water-free dry-cleaning solvents may be used for cleaning. Professional dry-cleaning is recommended.

SW   Either water-based cleaning agents, water-based foam, or mild, pure, water-free solvents may be used for cleaning. Professional cleaning is recommended.

X   Clean this fabric only by vacuuming or light brushing to remove overall soil.

WARNING: Do not use liquid cleaning agents of any type.

HOW TO CARE FOR FABRICS
Compiled by The Decorative Fabrics Association

1. FABRICS MUST BE PROTECTED FROM THE SUN. Draperies should be lined, and also interlined, when fragile fabrics are used. Shades should be drawn during the day, and awnings should be used whenever possible. Window glass magnifies the destructive elements in the rays of the sun. Winter sun and reflections from snow are even more harmful than summer sun. Strategically placed trees and shrubbery can help protect fabrics by shading your windows.

Colors can fade by oxidation—or "gas fading"—if fabrics are kept in storage for too long without airing. Some colors are more fugitive than others. Impurities in the air may cause as much fading as direct sunlight.

2. USE A REPUTABLE DRY-CLEANER that specializes in home furnishings. Dust has impurities that affect fabrics, so it is important to vacuum fabrics often, but clients should not try to remove excess spots themselves. Dry-cleaning should be done at regular intervals before excessive soil has accumulated. Very few fabrics are washable. Interior Designers can and should recommend professional dry-cleaning to their clients.

3. BE TOLERANT OF NORMAL FLUCTUATIONS in the lengths of draperies. Few fabrics are completely stable; fabrics breathe and absorb moisture, resulting in stretching or shrinking. It is reasonable to expect as much as a 3% change in any drapery length. In a 3-yard length (108 inches), this would amount to 3 inches up or down under various conditions. Fabrics placed over or near heating or cooling vents may react to a much greater degree.

4. FABRICS WEAR OUT. Some weaves are stronger than others, but none are indestructible. Wear will vary with the amount of use; unfortunately, a favorite chair will not last as long as a seldom-used show piece.

5. APPLIED FINISHES MAY HELP FABRICS resist soil and stain. Finishes help fabrics resist spotting, but they are not necessarily the end-all to every problem. For example, in general, light colors are likely to benefit from a finish, but dining room chairs will soil no matter what is used. A finish does not eliminate the necessity of properly caring for fabrics. Spots should still be given immediate attention by a professional dry-cleaner.

6. SYNTHETIC YARNS have made impressive strides in advancing the technology of weaving, but they cannot perform miracles. Performance will vary with the construction of the fabric and its application.

7. IT CANNOT BE TAKEN FOR GRANTED that, whether printed or woven, a fabric's pattern will be invariably "square" upon the cloth. Although in printing every effort is made to avoid distortion, occasionally it will exist. Therefore, when planning multiple-width fabrications, make certain before cutting that pattern alignment is adequate to produce a satisfactory result. This also applies to woven fabrics. Remember that all fabrics are subject to minor mis-weaves and other petty irregularities. Absolute perfection in textiles is virtually unattainable.

Chapter Two
Cutting New Foam Inserts & Drafting New Seat Cases with Piping

The following project discusses the construction of new foam inserts and new seat cases.

ABOUT THIS PROJECT:
FABRIC BY Woeller
PATTERN NAME Another Suede – Flax
FABRIC DIRECTION Regular
SEAT CUSHION YARDAGE 3.8 yards
TOTAL SOFA YARDAGE 10 yards

The cutting direction of Another Suede is regular, but after careful examination of the fabric and how it shades in all directions, I decided to cut this fabric in the railroaded direction. Running a fabric railroaded typically saves on yardage, but my interest in changing the direction was based on the elimination of seams. Had I cut the fabric in the regular direction, I would have had a seam on the center of the nose and a seam on the center of the OB.

In this particular color, the shading was similar in both the regular and railroaded direction, but in another color I may have come to a different conclusion. Some fabrics, like panne velvet, will be cut in the direction that shades most. Whether for practical or aesthetic reasons, there are times when you may decide to change the direction of your fabric.

Foam

With age, all foam will begin to disintegrate and powder. Exposure to direct sun will accelerate this process. If your furniture requires new foam on the IB or IA, or requires spring repair, I suggest that you reupholster your furniture, rather than slipcover. If you plan to slipcover with the intention of reupholstering at a later time, a loose-fitting, casual slipcover will guarantee that your cover will fit after your furniture has been reupholstered.

With time foam will decompress, and gaps may appear between the seat cushions or along the IA. Seat cushions may also recede away from the front of the nose. If any of the above conditions describe your seat cushions, it is time to replace your seat foam, and you should do so *before* cutting a new seat case from fabric.

When buying foam, I recommend buying from an upholstery shop rather than a mass retailer. Good foam is expensive and mass retailers' typically stock lower grades for prices similar to better quality foams available through upholstery shops. Qualux® and Ultracell® are two leading foam brands that you should look for. Do not be dismayed by the price of good foam; even if you do not keep your furniture, the seat foam can be removed, re-cut, and glued again.

Typically, soft foam should be used for the IB only. You should choose medium or firm foam for seating. Anyone with back or hip discomfort should not sit on soft foam because pressure will be placed on the body due to mis-alignment.

Common Seat Shapes

Measure your seat dimensions carefully. Your cushions may look square, but often they are not.

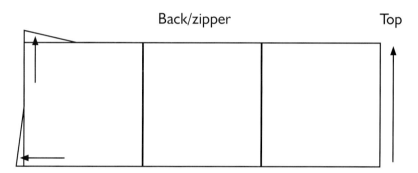

Seat cushions may curve out to fill the sides or the corners into the IB. The top arrow indicates the pattern layout when cutting.

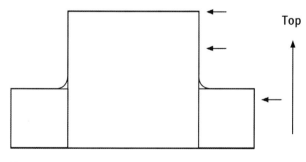

T-cushion.

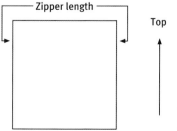

Foam inserts require that zipper bands be sewn down the sides of a seat case.

The width of a T-cushion often varies along several points, as indicated by the arrows. the back corners of a T-cushion cannot be cut in one piece; the first possible seam must be located in teh curve area of the "T". Additional bands can be cut on each side to reach the zipper band.

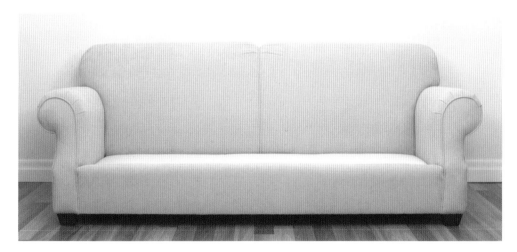

TO REVIVE OLDER FOAM, simply remove the poly batting and steam the foam over an electric kettle, rotating the foam over the spout. When the foam has dried, poly wrap will be glued to the foam. This method is not a replacement for new foam, but your foam will have a fresher, fuller appearance.

Keeping Your Original Foam Inserts

If you are cutting a new seat case but keeping the original foam, cross reference all measurements when drafting a pattern for fabric. Measure within the frame of your furniture, and compare those measurements to both sides of the original seat case. If you are not in the habit of regularly turning seat cases, one seat top may have stretched significantly. It is preferable to rely on frame measurements to cut new foam inserts, however, measuring the original seat case will give you insight into how the seat case was styled.

My Foam Measurements

Measure arm to arm, and divide results according to the number of seat cushions. My total width is 69.25"; I have two seat cushions, so each will measure 34.75" wide. The depth of my seat is 22.5". My foam is cut perfectly square, and my fabric pattern is cut from the identical measurements, plus SA. To measure the depth of the seat, place a ruler against the IB, along the deck.

If you are cutting new foam inserts, you can change the depth of your seat to your preference. I like to cut cushions so that the legs stay off of the nose in the sitting position. This will greatly reduce wear and keep fabrics clean. My foam inserts are anywhere from ½" to 1" over the edge of the nose. Because foam compresses with age, this method will also extend the life of your furniture.

When cutting new foam inserts, remove the cushions to measure the deck depth.

Once your foam is cut and shaped, place it on your furniture to test the dimensions. If you wish to make changes to the depth, glue more foam along the back, or trim off a little at a time. If you are working with a T-cushion and are having trouble establishing the depth, you may have to cut off the ends and glue on new "T" pieces. Do not panic if you do not get it right the first time; cutting new foam takes a keen eye, and foam can always be salvaged with glue.

Drafting the Seat Pattern

Once you have decided on the shape of your insert, you can cut the seat cushion from fabric. You will use the foam only as a guide to cut your seat pattern. **IMPORTANT!** When drafting your pattern on your fabric, rely on measurements; do not trace the outline of your foam on your fabric. You may have measured carefully, but cutting the foam may have resulted in uneven edges.

For most fabrics, cutting the piping at 1.5" wide usually results in .5" of SA. If your fabric is very thick, cutting the piping at 1.5" usually results in 3/8" of SA. The resultant affect on SA affects not only the seat components, but the SA for the whole project wherever piping is sewn. Test your fabric by making a small piping sample before drafting your pattern. If a piping test results in 3/8" of SA, the seat top, band and zipper bands will be drafted with 3/8" of SA.

Of course adjustments can be made, and piping width can be adjusted. The minimum piping width should be 1 3/8" for lightweight fabrics.

For a basic seat case, the finished height of the band is the thickness of the foam. A 4" foam insert will require a 5" seat band, assuming that the SA is .5".

I always cut my zipper band with a 1" fold on the side that the zipper is sewn.

How Poly Batting can Change a Pattern

The original seat foam on this sofa measured 4.5" thick, and the seat band was finished at 5.5". In place of standard poly batting, a thick 1" batting, pictured below, was inserted on both sides of the foam to create a lofty pile. The total foam and batting measurement equals 6.5", creating a lofty pile when the batting compresses inside of the case. Because the foam thickness is not equivalent to the seat band height, this method of pattern development usually results in a casual, relaxed look with time.

The diagram below illustrates another way that fill materials affect the pattern.

This type of seat pattern is typically drafted with an additional .75" at midpoint, and then smoothed into the corners. In contrast, the foam insert is cut with 90-degree angles, and the foam thickness is greater than the seat band height. For example, the foam thickness may be 7", versus a 5.5" finished seat band height. This method does achieve a high loft; however, it also results in poor wear as it contributes to seam slippage and fabric stretching. This is largely due to the necessity of a soft foam insert to create this style. It would be very difficult to insert a 7" piece of foam into a seat case with a 5.5" band if the foam was firm.

If your seat case is not square, it may have been cut using this method. Since it can be difficult to measure older cases after fabric has stretched, look for clues by observing the grain of your fabric.

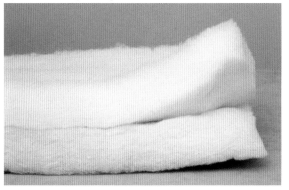 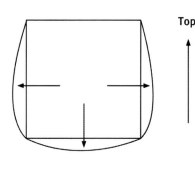

Top

The original poly batting.

How My Seat Case Was Cut

- The foam inserts were cut at 34.75" x 22.5" x 2 pieces.
- The new foam thickness is 5", the finished seat band is 5".
- The seat band was cut at 6", which allows for .5" SA on either side.
- The foam was covered with one square of batting and one continuous wrap*
- With SA, the fabric seat top pattern measures 35.75" x 23.5" deep x 4 pieces.
- Each seat top requires 118" of piping at 1.5".
- The cushion band length is 6" x 59" x 2 pieces.
- The zipper length is 4" x 59" x 4 pieces.

* Refer to basic wrapping techniques found on page (**XX**)

When calculating the width for the zipper band, divide the finished band width by two. Add 1" on the zipper side, and .5" SA to be sewn to the case. Using these measurements, the yardage estimate for two seat cases in the railroaded direction is 3.8 yards. When a seat band is very narrow, you may want to decrease the zipper allowance on the zipper band so that it does not get caught in the seam on the case side.

Piping Assembly

In upholstered furniture, the piping cord is usually made of paper. If you plan to wash your slipcover, you must purchase cotton piping cord. Paper cord will be stiffer, but the main reason it is used in manufacturing is cost, as the cotton cord is a little more expensive. Purchase a good quality cord; the diameter should be solid and consistent, as the quality of the cord will greatly affect the finished product. The standard cord size used in furniture manufacturing is 5/32", or 0.4 cm. This cord will be commonly referred to as "piping cord" in the garment trade, but in the furniture trade, "welting" or "welting cord" is the common name. Both terms refer to the same product.

As shown on the following page, there are two ways to assemble piping fabric, as you will rarely be able to cut one continuous length of piping.

Good quality piping should be consistent in diameter.

Once the lengths of piping have been assembled, fold the fabric over the piping cord and sew with a piping foot or zipper foot.

If you are sewing a very thin fabric, you may find that a standard piping foot will not sew a tight piping cord. When the purchase of a smaller piping foot does not suffice, you may have to use Teflon® tape to fill the piping channel. In commercial production, feet are machined to precise measurements.

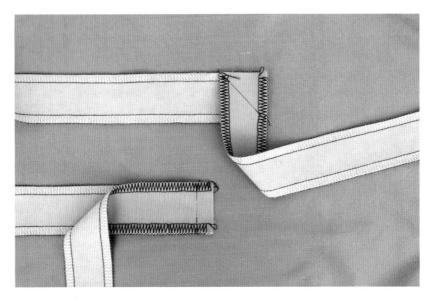

The two methods of sewing continuous piping.

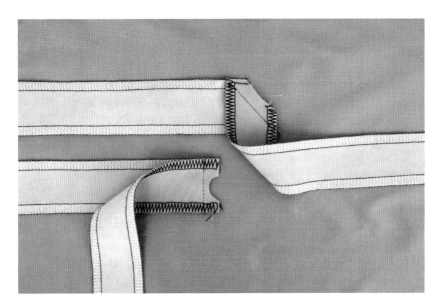

With heavier weight fabrics, cut into the SA to reduce bulk.

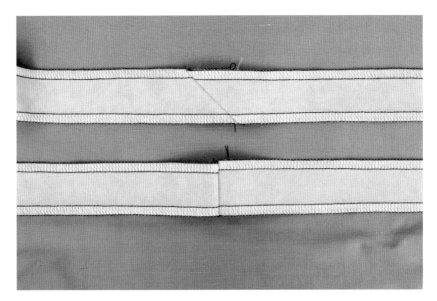

The finished seam.

Continuous Zipper

Continuous zipper is sold on rolls, and the zipper pulls are often purchased separately. The tape of continuous zipper is printed with arrows. Start the zipper pull at the end of the tape which shows the top of the arrow.

Sewing Order

1. Once the seat, piping, band, and zipper have been cut, overlock all pieces.
2. Assemble the zipper band
3. Assemble the piping cord.
4. Sew the piping around both seat tops.
5. Sew the band and zipper to one seat top.
6. Assemble to the 2nd seat top.

Basic Wrapping Techniques

The zipper band assembly.

If a seat case is pulled over a foam insert without poly batting, the resulting look is flat and lifeless. Poly batting adds the finishing touch to seat cushions. Here are the basic wrapping techniques that can be used with standard batting for regular seat construction. These techniques donot require a pattern change. For regular or standard seat construction, the foam height always equals the finished band height.

If you are interested in higher loft, refer to the note, "How Poly Batting can Change a Pattern. For regular seat construction, these techniques do not require a pattern change. For regular or standard seat construction, the foam height always equals the finished band height.

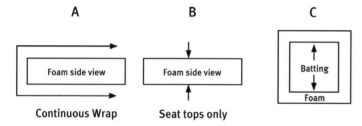

Basic wrapping techniques, which do not require a pattern change.

Example B in the diagram illustrates how poly batting is glued on the top of both surfaces. In this method, be sure that extra glue is applied around the cushion edges, as the wrap does not continue over the front of the seat.

In example C, a smaller square of batting is glued to the top of the foam, and then wrapped a second time in either method A or B.

Wrapping is never glued to the foam along the back of the cushion.

Both methods A and B can be used alone, and C is always followed by either A or B.

The Assembled Seat Case

Be sure to notch your pattern pieces and check frequently before finishing the entire assembly. If your seat case does not sit naturally square, but twists instead, then the corners of both seat tops are not in line with each other on the seat band.

If that is correct, check that your zipper band and seat band have been cut and sewn square. This area is usually the second source of the problem.

After inserting foam into seat cases, you may notice pockets of air in the corners. This is normal in all upholstery applications and quickly remedied with a tuft of poly fill.

Chapter Three
Pattern Changes for Foam and Loose Fill

The following project discusses the process of working without existing cushions as a reference, and how a basic pattern for loose fill differs from a basic pattern for foam.

ABOUT THIS PROJECT:
FABRIC BY Waverly
COLLECTION Waverly Sun-N-Shade
PATTERN NAME Rodeo Drive – Sea Spray
SKU NO. 669250
HORIZONTAL REPEAT 4.5"
FABRIC DIRECTION Regular
FABRIC WIDTH 54"
SEAT CUSHION YARDAGE 3.1 yards

The Frame and the Seating Position

I chose the materials and construction of my cushions to accommodate my natural reclining position. When modifying a pattern, or building from scratch, seat depth, back height, and their effect on posture are all factors that should influence design details.

The dimensions of this bench forced either an upright position, or the tendency to slide toward the edge of the seat. Sitting on the seat edge of foam inserts would have caused both the foam and the seat case to twist excessively. With this in mind, the following pattern decisions were made.

The IB cushion height was cut to fit into the curve of the back, so that the upper body would not be pushed forward. The pattern was cut as a basic cushion because it would occupy the least amount of space.

The seat cushion was cut with a band that measures only 2". The top height of the bench and its position on the back influenced this decision. Sitting on a higher cushion elevates your position, and in this case, the top rail would have caused discomfort on the back. I chose to use the washable synthetic, down-like product called Ball Fiber™, for the loose fill.

Loose Fill

Cushions filled with a loose fill product, including down, requires a pattern that differs from foam. Because loose fill lifts and pulls in cases, patterns are required to be slightly larger than foam patterns. Different case styles call for further changes as well. In this example, I used the same fill product for both the IB and seat cushion, but the fill allowance for the two pattern styles is not identical.

Loose fill patterns can differ not only with the type of product used, but by the amount used as well. If you would like to overstuff your cushions, patterns will need to be cut even larger. When using foam, a pattern can be cut from exact measurements taken from a frame. Unless it is your desired effect, cutting a pattern from exact measurements and using loose fill instead of foam will leave gaps between cushions.

If you are using loose fill, and are uncomfortable cutting yardage directly, I suggest you use an inexpensive cloth for a test.

Ball Fiber™.

How a Print Influences Layout

Without a nose or skirt to consider, I concentrated on how the pattern would continue along the back of the bench. I have decided to use two different case styles with a print which must line up, and now I must decide which stripe will be used as my center.

Because the IB cushion was cut in a basic pattern, I did not want the primary stripe to fall and hide into the folds at the center of the bench. This was the deciding factor in the layout of the print. The blue stripe would be used as the center, specifically so that the primary stripe would not fall in the center of the bench.

Had both the seat and the IB cases been cut in a box-cushion style, I could have centered the primary stripe at the center of the bench, half of the stripe on each side of the bench. For a three seat sofa, the center seat cushion and center IB cushion are the guides which affect the layout of a pattern throughout an entire project. When working with a loveseat, the center of the seat cushion is the guide which affects the layout of a pattern.

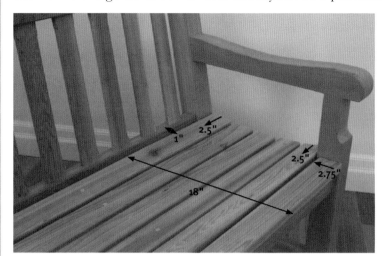

Lay a soft tape along the curve of the seat to measure the seat depth.

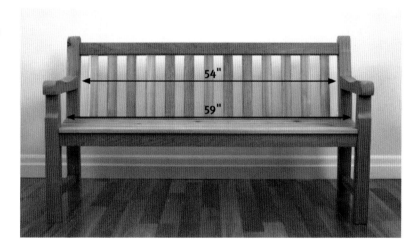

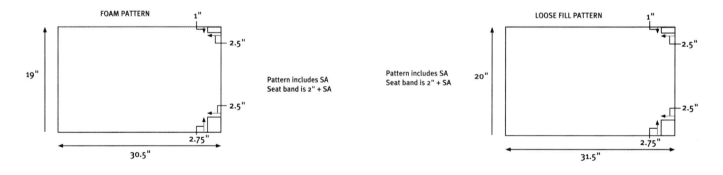

The pattern measurements for foam inserts vs. loose fill.

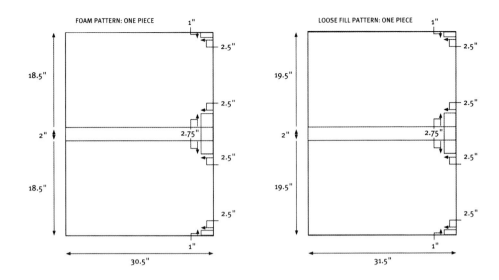

The seat case can be cut in one piece.

The diagram illustrates how this seat case can be cut in one piece if the seat band is factored into the pattern. Side bands and a zipper would be sewn in to complete the seat case. The center of the seat band, which is 2", would be the match point for the center of the side band. The side band would be cut at 3" to include SA. SA is included in the patterns.

Drafting a Pattern from Measurements

The stripe of our pattern, Rodeo Drive, was cut in two directions on the seat case. If you would like to feature one direction only, the seat case can be cut in one continuous piece. The seat top height for the loose fill cushion cut in one piece is 19.5". This calculation is made by increasing the pattern .5" along the front and .5" along the back for fill allowance. An additional .5" is added along the back for the zipper SA. The seat band is factored into the pattern, so all SA along the front is eliminated. The loose fill IB cushion measures 10" in height, including SA. The total width of the IB cushion is 30", including SA. The width is calculated by dividing the width of the bench in two: 27", + 1" allowance on each end of the cushion, plus a total of 1" SA.

Unlike a foam insert, the zipper band for a loose fill case filled with Ball Fiber™ does not have to come down the sides of the case. This loose fill product is down-like, and can be inserted into the seat case without causing any pressure on the zipper or the seams. Using these measurements, the center of the IB is 15" and the center of the seat is 14.5". The center points on both patterns will be laid over the center of the blue stripe when cutting.

IMPORTANT! Remember to cut an opposite, or mirror image, and mark the top of your pattern. The cutouts on this pattern are not symmetrical. If you are working with a pattern that needs to be centered, or a fabric that has an obvious direction, another pattern would have to be cut if the pattern is mistakenly rotated.

Pattern Placement for the Horizontal Stripe

I cut the stripe on the seat band in the horizontal direction. After deciding how I would like to center the stripe on the seat band, I can continue the stripe up into the seat top. To continue the stripe, you must begin to draft the seat top where the finished band ends, and then add SA.

The inserts can be cut with the same pattern measurements used for the seat case.

The seat top on the reverse side was cut in the horizontal direction.

24

Chapter Four
Headboard Slipcover

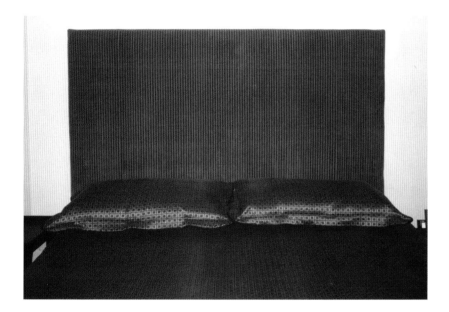

```
ABOUT THIS PROJECT:
FABRIC BY Woeller
PATTERN NAME Cord – Artichoke
FABRIC DIRECTION Regular
YARDAGE 3.4 yards
```

Working with a Nap

Any fabric with a nap needs to be cut in the same direction throughout a project. If components are cut in different directions, shading will occur. This is applicable to all textiles, in all applications, from furniture to garments. Most fabrics with a nap will be cut so that the pile runs down. This means that the arrow on the pattern indicating the top would run against the nap. To find the top of your fabric run the open palm of your hand up and down your yardage. In the opposite direction, the pile will stand up. For some fabrics establishing the direction of a pile may take time. Using chalk, always indicate the top of all components and assemble them so that the nap lies flat when seams are sewn. If you sew against the nap, raising the pile, you will create a seam that puckers.

SEWING

Many textiles have very specific adjustments that need to be made for trouble-free sewing. Velvet, for example, is a textile that needs extra preparation and time during assembly. Sewing machines are normally very accommodating when sewing medium-weight fabrics with stable properties. If your machine is not properly maintained, sewing fabrics with atypical qualities is a test that your machine may not pass.

Refer to this basic checklist if you are experiencing any sewing difficulties.

- ☐ Are you using the correct needle size?
- ☐ Is your needle fresh? Replace your needle as soon as signs of wear show. A general rule is after 8 hours of use.
- ☐ Is your thread tension properly set for the fabric you are sewing?
- ☐ Are you sewing with a good quality thread? Your thread should not curl when coming off of a spool.
- ☐ Are the feed dogs on your machine worn out?
- ☐ Are the feet on your machine worn out?
- ☐ Make sure that the bobbin thread can be pulled smoothly and does not snag. Any burrs around the needle plate must be filed with emery cord. Hold the emery cord taut, just as you would dental floss. You must remove the casing under the bobbin area in order to pass the cord up through the throat plate. Emery cord should be available where industrial sewing machines are sold.
- ☐ Be wary of inexpensive sewing attachments. Price reflects quality. The quality of pins and springs in sewing machine feet will affect how the fabric is fed. If the sewing foot does not sit level under pressure, your fabric will not be fed straight.

Emery cord.

Headboard Slipcover

    This slipcover pattern was not draped on the headboard; it was drafted from measurements taken from the frame. Depending on the weave and yarn of your fabric, a textile may "give" across the width, and you may decide to make adjustments after assembly. To accommodate the width of this headboard, two seams were added, and in most cases an adjustment could be made along these seams. However, because the pattern of this fabric cannot be interrupted, any alteration would involve disassembly and an adjustment to the pattern in the corners to decrease the width across the headboard.

    Whether you build a headboard or have one custom made, it will have to be upholstered in an intermediate fabric. I used double-sided flannel, which is used as an interlining in drapery. The building layers were foam, poly batting, and then double-sided flannel.

    To draft a pattern, you need to know the following:

- *The thickness of the foam (in our case, 3")*
- *The thickness of the frame (.75")*
- *The width of Velcro® tape that you will use (2")*
- *The headboard measurements (77"w x 48"h)*
- *The width of the fabric (54")*
- *The direction of the fabric (Regular)*

    According to the frame and fabric measurements, the finished slipcover will consist of three separate pieces, one for the headboard and one for each of the two legs. Again, two seams will be added on the headboard to accommodate the width. The seam lines are indicated in the pattern as a dotted line. This fabric and all stripes offer the perfect opportunity to hide seams.

    If the headboard was to be sewn with a band, the total front panel would equal 77" x 48", plus SA. In this example, the corners are mitered and the cover continues to the back seamlessly, without a band. The total width necessary is 77" plus 5.75" on both ends. This amount includes the thickness of the foam, which is 3", the width of the Velcro® tape, which is 2", and the frame thickness, which is .75".

    An additional 2" of SA is needed across the width to assemble the three panels of the headboard. To summarize:

- *The legs were covered individually.*
- *The leg height is 20", the width is 10". The yardage needed for each leg is 22" x 12".*
- *The total width of yardage needed is 90.5".*
- *The length of fabric needed is 48" + 5.75" + 5.75", for a total of 59.5".*

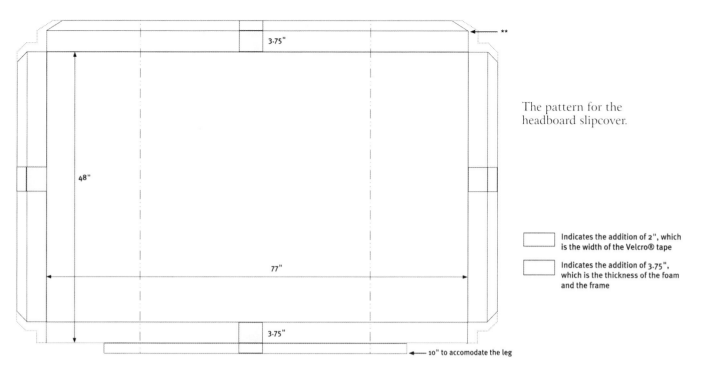

3·75"

48"

77"

3·75"

← 10" to accomodate the leg

The pattern for the headboard slipcover.

Indicates the addition of 2", which is the width of the Velcro® tape

Indicates the addition of 3.75", which is the thickness of the foam and the frame

The dotted red line indicates the addition of .5" SA.

All raw edges are overlocked, except the green area, which is finished with binding. The green line is level with the mattress. When sewn, it is flush with the back of the frame. **NOTE:** When the mitered corner is sewn, this point sits on the outer edge of the frame, against the wall.

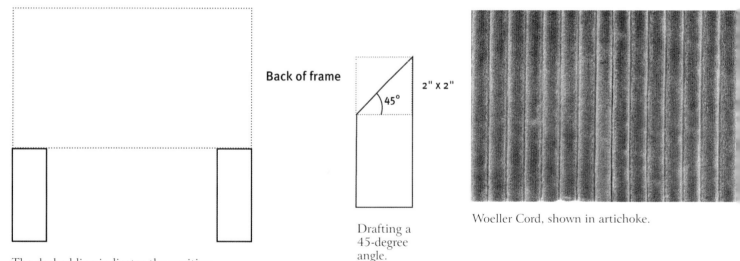

Back of frame

2" X 2"

45°

The dashed line indicates the position of the Velcro® tape on the back of the frame.

Drafting a 45-degree angle.

Woeller Cord, shown in artichoke.

The dashed line in the first diagram indicates the position of the Velcro® tape on the back of the frame. Velcro® tape also runs down the sides of both legs.

The second diagram illustrates the method of creating a mitered corner. In order to do so, a 45-degree angle needs to be drafted. To draft a 45-degree angle, map a 2" square and draw a line corner to corner. Remember to add SA. As long as the boxed measurement is square, a 45-degree angle can be drafted using this method.

To better understand how the slipcover pattern is drafted and finished you can cut and sew a small scale model. Use a headboard measurement of 13" wide by 8" in height, which is approximately a 1/6 scale. Use the same allowance of 5.75" to continue the headboard towards the back, and cut in 1.75" to accommodate the leg.

Chapter Five
Bergere Chair

ABOUT THIS PROJECT:
FABRIC BY Waverly
COLLECTION Waverly Remember When
PATTERN NAME Stripe – Lake
SKU NO. 648883
VERTICAL REPEAT 0.125"
HORIZONTAL REPEAT 3.375"
FABRIC DIRECTION Regular
FABRIC WIDTH 54"
YARDAGE 5 yards (One yard has been reserved for the 2" bias used to make the binding.)

Once decisions have been made about how a pattern will be centered, measure the frame to locate the center points for draping. If you are working with furniture that is upholstered in a print, do not use the existing upholstery as a guide to center the pattern of your slipcover. Always measure the width of the frame, locate the center points, and insert pins into the upholstery. When draping a pattern that requires centering, feel for the pins, and place the center of the blocks over them.

Draping the Bib

Feeling for the pins, place the center of the pattern, over the pins, and then pin the fabric into the upholstery. I finished the edge of my bib with binding, so I used the outer edge of the double-welt on the chair to outline the pattern of my bib.

Next, determine the position of the ties and sew them in temporarily. Return the bib to the chair to determine if the ties are in the best position to keep the bib upright.

The top two tabs of the bib and one tab above one arm is sewn in permanently. The tab above the other arm opens with a tiny piece of Velcro®. Under each arm, the ties are permanently sewn to the bib and they come together to make a bow. The back pattern is the same shape as the front, except for the slight curve that accommodates the arm on the front. In this area, the back was cut straight.

If a fabric lacks body or needs support to stay upright, a fusible backing can be used and should be applied before the binding is sewn to the bib.

This binding was cut 2" wide on the bias. Assemble the strips of bias as shown. With an iron, quarter the bias tape until you have a binding that is .5" wide.

Preparing the bias binding.

The center of the stripe is placed on the center of the frame. Relief cuts are used to release the fabric around the arm. A relief cut can be made directly into the corner, as shown on the left, or in the center of the arm, and then into the corners.

The finished bib with temporary ties.

IB Cushion: Using Markers to Draft a Pattern

Using a soft tape measure, you will take measurements from the IB cushion and transfer them onto a paper pattern that will be used to cut the fabric. Measurements are always taken seam-to-seam, never to the edge of the piping cord. After the pattern has been drafted on paper, SA can be added. It is critical to be observant and accurate in order to duplicate the cushion styling.

Using these measurements, I can draft a pattern.

The width across the cushion at the base	*25"*
The height of the cushion	*19.5"*
The width of the case 3" down from the cushion top	*22.5"*
The band depth	*1"*
The finished length of the zipper	*23"*

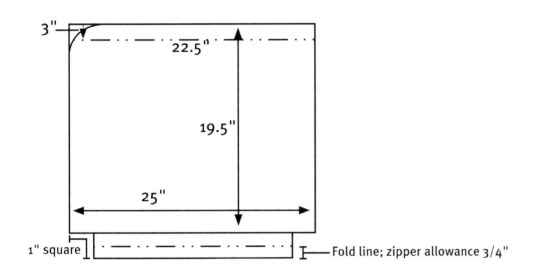

Drafting the IB cushion from measurements.

Because you are measuring from seam to seam, the pattern in the diagram does not include SA.

In the corner marked 1" square, a SA of 3/8" is standard, even if you have allocated a .5" SA around the perimeter of the case. In the top corners, the fabric pattern will be cut straight; the curve will be established in the draping process. The pleat size and location is also best determined during the draping. Once the pattern is cut, drape the pattern over the cushion and pin into the SA at the piping. The final cushion height was decreased by 2.5" to display the bib detail. I also chose to eliminate the corner pleat; this is easily accomplished by cutting a slight amount of fabric out of the curve.

Drape the IB over the cushion to determine the shape of the curve, the pleat position, and the size.

Once the corner, illustrated as 1" square, is sewn, the band width on the bottom of the cushion is formed. When assembled, the band width for this cushion is 2". The length of the cushion, 23", is also the length across the back of the seat cushion, from corner to corner. If you prefer to increase the band width for the IB cushion, the 1" square measurement would increase outward, and would need to remain square. The finished length of 23", shown as the zipper fold line, needs to remain constant, because it fills the width of the chair at the base of the cushion. Changing the band width affects the seating position. If you have a shallow seat, you will have less room in which to recline. The pattern change will also affect the shape of the cushion between the arms, because the new depth will have to smooth into the arm area. If you are unsure about changes, make a sample pattern in muslin to develop a new pattern.

Sewing Assembly for the IB Cushion

Fold back the .75" zipper allowance and sew in the zipper (represented by the dotted line in the illustration on the previous page).

Sew the piping cord around the perimeter of one cushion. Sew the 2nd cushion to the assembly around the perimeter.

At this point the entire case is sewn except for the corners, which form the cushion base. Reverse the case and line up the center of the zipper to the piping. Reinforce the area over the zipper teeth with a scrap of material and sew straight across from corner to corner.

Seat Cushion: Using Markers to Draft a Pattern

Use the same method to draft the seat cushion. Assess your chair and pattern to find the markers that will help you draft a pattern.

Seat width at zipper.	23"
Measure the distance from center back cushion to first instep...	16 3/8"
... and the width of the seat at this point.	29"
Measure the complete length from the back to the front	24.5"
Draw a soft tape from corner to corner along the cushion front. In the center insert a pin into the cushion. Measure the distance from the pin to the front of the cushion.	1.5"
Measure the width of the cushion from corner to corner.	29
Measure the height of the "T"	4"
Measure the instep	2"
Measure the height of the cutout	2.5 "

Cross reference your measurements for accuracy. The distance from B to C should be the sum of 2.5 + 4 + 1.5.

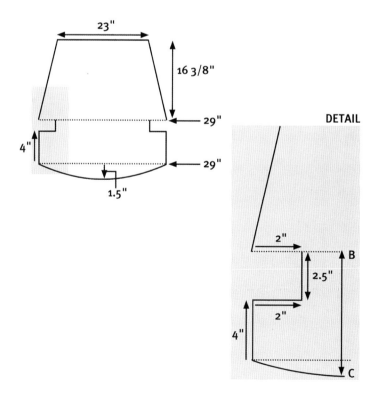

Drafting the seat cushion from measurements.

When drafting any pattern for a cushion, always cross-reference your numbers with the deck and frame whenever possible. This chair is a good example of a frame that cannot be easily referenced. The arm slopes towards the back, and the cutout accommodates the arm at the deck level and 5" above the deck.

Although a foam insert can be used as a reference, many Bergere chairs are filled with down or down-like materials. The seat inserts can be cut much longer than the total length of the seat case and built with baffle walls. This is yet another method of construction that creates loft, and the longer length fills the corners without leaving pockets of air.

Before the side cushion band can be cut and sewn, a point of reference is needed to center the stripe.

1. Begin by returning the original seat cushion to the chair.
2. Measure the side length of the chair, from the edge of the back leg to the front corner of the frame.
3. Indicate the center of this measurement by inserting a pin into the upholstery.
4. Transfer this center point up onto the original seat band and then onto the seat cushion. It is the center of the stripe on this seat band, which lines up to this notch.
5. After indicating this mark on the cushion, measure the distance to the back corner of the seat case.
6. From the corner, transfer the distance of this notch onto your seat top pattern while allocating for SA.

The seam joining the front and side band will be hidden behind the arm. The seat cushion should be fully assembled and sewn before the skirt

Place the original seat cushion on the chair and measure from the back edge of the leg to the front of the chair to find the center for the skirt. Transfer this point onto the seat band, then onto the seat case. Line the center of the stripe to this notch, and the pattern on the side band will line up with the skirt.

Draping the Deck

Measure the widest points of the deck, and cut a block that will be used to drape the deck. (Refer to the wingback slipcover in chapter six).

Place the block on the deck so that the relief cuts can be made. Cut carefully, pulling your fabric back and cutting along the frame. After all of the relief cuts have been made, pin the deck into the upholstery in preparation to drape the skirt. Allow the deck fabric to drape naturally, smoothing the fabric into place tautly, but not overly tight. Remember that the deck will compress when the chair is occupied.

Relief cuts on the deck.

Relief cuts on the deck.

After the relief cuts have been made, the deck can be cut around the frame.

Draping the Skirt

The deck area on most upholstered furniture is even and consistent; the *opposite* is true for a Bergere chair. For this reason, fitting a skirt to hang properly can be time consuming and will require patience. Because the curve along the front nose can be hollow, draping a shorter skirt length will ensure that the skirt will hang at its best.

On the deck, the skirt should come up under the seat cushion far enough so that the deck material is not visible from a standing position. If you cannot bring the skirt back far enough, a separate panel will need to be sewn onto the deck. A narrow bias panel along the front of the chair will probably be sufficient.

In extreme cases, if your skirt does not fall or fill nicely, you may want to sew fill materials into your skirt where needed. Crinoline, felt, or lambswool, which is used in dressmaking to fill the area at the end of a shoulder pad, are some possible materials.

Assemble the skirt and the skirt lining. Press, then stitch and overlock along the top of the skirt length. With the assembled seat cushion on the chair, begin by pinning the skirt into the chair. The hem of the skirt should measure the same distance from the floor up, all around the chair. As you pin, smooth the deck taut into position, while still allowing the fabric to drape along the deck naturally. When the entire skirt has been draped, indicate its position around the perimeter of the deck, and indicate notches on both the deck and the skirt, then sew into place. The skirt is sewn to the deck just as it is draped, without allocating SA.

This deck was finished in bias binding that continues into the skirt. The skirt closes with hooks that were sewn in by hand. The finished height of this skirt is 5.5".

Refer to the wingback slipcover in chapter six for details on skirt assembly.

Draping the skirt into position.

The skirt should come up onto the deck far enough so that the deck is not visible under the seat cushion. Note that the deck sits naturally in the crevice of the upholstered deck.

Draping the Top Arm

The outer pleat located at the front of the arm is the largest pleat, and the three remaining pleats are all equal in size. Therefore, the RSF top arm must be cut an as opposite, or mirror.

If your fabric is a match, indicate the top of the pattern so that the second piece is not accidentally rotated when it is cut. When the arms have been sewn, mark the front of each cover "LF" and "RF" to ensure that once removed they are returned to their proper positions. Each cover was finished with 2" binding, and four pieces of narrow, 4mm black elastic were sewn to each cover. Form a knot on either side under the arm—not in the center of the arm—and tuck the elastic ends under the arm piece.

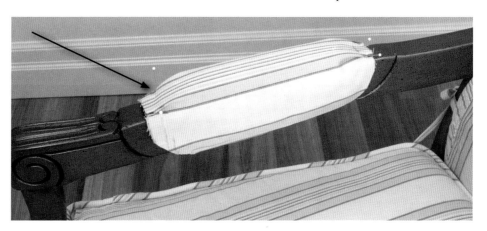

Draping the top arm.

Negotiating Curves

When assembling a straight seat band to a seat top with a front curve, it is unlikely that the patterns will line up perfectly. The distance from center stripe to center stripe on a curve will be longer. If a curve is slight, or a fabric gives, it may be possible to match a small repeat.

Chapter Six
Wingback Chair

ABOUT THIS PROJECT:
FABRIC BY Waverly
COLLECTION Williamsburg Tidewater
Collection Vol. 1
PATTERN NAME Indienne – Indigo
SKU NO. 665230
VERTICAL REPEAT 16"*
HORIZONTAL REPEAT 13.5"*
FABRIC DIRECTION Regular
FABRIC WIDTH 54"
YARDAGE 7.25 yards
SKIRT LINING 1.6 yards / regular
direction

*Although the repeat pattern is listed, Indienne was
cut as an allover pattern. This lively fabric proves that
matching a pattern is not always necessary.

Calculating Yardage

Yardage is calculated after all design decisions have been made and the fabric has been chosen. Using a soft tape measure, you will list each component in your furniture and the corresponding measurements. These measurements, called blocks, are used to drape the slipcover. All SA is accounted for when taking these measurements, and you must be certain of the the grain direction for each component, as this will affect the yardage estimate. For all blocks except the seat and skirt, add a few extra inches in each direction. The following questions should be answered before calculating yardage:

- The fabric width
- The cutting direction; is it regular or railroaded?
- Is the fabric a match?
- The skirt height
- Where the skirt will drop from

When you have your final yardage estimate, add a minimum of a half-yard allowance. This will give you some play for both error and fabric imperfections.

The following is a list of block measurements for this slipcover:

- IB To determine the IB height, measure to the deck and add 5" tucking fabric. *Height 41", Width 38"*

- OB I have already decided to add a skirt on the slipcover, and it will drop from the deck. This block measurement reflects that decision. Measuring from the floor, transfer the height of the skirt onto the back of the chair for an approximate seam line. *Height 33", Width 29"*

- IW *Height 25", Width 15"*

- OW *Height 22", Width 15"*

- IA Measure to the deck and add 5" for the tucking fabric. *Height 29", Width 29"*

- OA This measurement reflects the decision to drop the skirt from the deck. The OA is not measured to the bottom of the frame. *Height 9.5", Width 30"*

- Arm Front *Height 16", Width 6"*

- Seat *Height 23", Width 23"*

  - Seat band *Height 5", Width 59"*
  - Zipper *3.5" x 37"*

- Skirt

  - Skirt height *14"*
  - Front skirt *28" + 8" fold (36")*
  - Side skirt *29" + 8" fold (37"), x 2*

- Back skirt *23" + 8" fold (31")*

- Deck *Height 12", Width 26"*

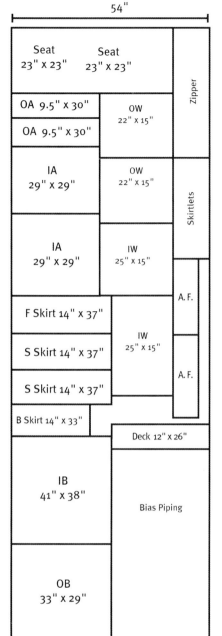

On paper, plot a yardage estimate using the block measurements within the fabric width. It is not necessary to make an immediate allowance for the piping. After mapping out your blocks, more often than not you will have a place where the piping can be cut. This is true for the skirtlets, as well.

The piping on the skirt and seat were cut in the regular direction, and all of the remaining piping was cut on the bias.

The calculated yardage is 6.7 yards, plus .5 yard allowance, for a total of 7.25 yards.

The zipper was cut cross-grain to utilize the yardage.

Draping the IW and OW

In upholstery, fabric can be coaxed and eased into place. Furthermore, the use of fill materials to smooth out lines means that styling an upholstered piece is less troublesome than creating a slipcover. For these reasons, the OW and IW curves and style lines are always corrected on a slipcover. These changes will ensure that the cover sits in a natural, relaxed position without twisting or needing constant adjustment. As well, moving the right seams will help a slipcover mimic the look of upholstery.

Drape and pin the IW block into place, make sure that you will have enough fabric to work with in every direction.

Fold the fabric back to make the relief cuts. A relief cut will release the tucking fabric into the chair, and allow the top corner of the wing to sit in position.

Relief cuts on the IW.

Plotting a yardage estimate using blocks.

The completed fitting of the IW.

Smooth the fabric into the tucking area to determine the tucking amount. Pull the fabric out and immediately cut off any excess tucking fabric.

Fold and pin the pleats along the front of the IW.

The most critical change in the arm assembly is at the point where the seams of the IW, OW, and IA all meet in the slipcover, as indicated on the following page by the arrow "X".

Once this point has been identified a new style line will be outlined along the IW using seam tape or another suitable tape. Make corrections along the length of the wing until the new style line looks natural and pleasing.

The new style line for the slipcover runs along the break line, just where the fabric would be pulled around towards the back of the chair.

Reshaping the IW. This photo illustrates the new pattern line from the front.

A closer look at the most critical change for the arm assembly.

Drape the OW, keeping a straight grain. The straight grain is always perpendicular to the floor. Along the tape, fold the fabric of the OW under and outline the IW and OW seam line. Transfer the pleat positions onto the OW, and notch the OW and IW to ensure accuracy during assembly.

Remove the OW and IW; add SA and assemble. The bias piping cord will be sewn to the OW, and then assembled to the IW. Be sure to use the length of the OW to calculate the piping length. The longer length of piping cord will facilitate the final assembly for the OB and OA, as illustrated on page 47.

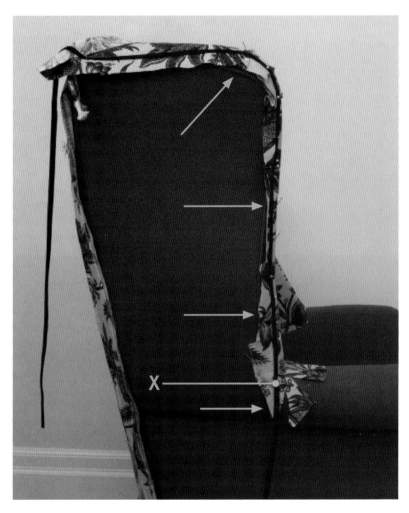

The arrows indicate the upholstered seam line – a sharp contrast to the slipcover seam line outlined with black tape. The shape of the slipcover outline is redrawn into the point marked "X". Identifying this point is the most important change for the arm assembly in a slipcover.

Draping the OW. The pleat position and notches have been transferred to both the IW and OW.

Draping the IB and OB

Typically, zippers are sewn along frame corners, but the shape of this OB allowed a straight cut that would run right into the corner. That opportunity and a vibrant print ensured that one longer zipper could be used discreetly.

Sew the zipper into the OB block, drape and outline the OB.

Remove; add SA and overlock.

Sew the piping along the top seam of the OB and return to the chair. The piping cord is sewn first to any component which lays flat against the upholstery. The IB, which needs to be eased over the upholstery, will be eased into the OB along this seam.

The OB is prepared for the IB to be draped.

When the wings have been assembled, return them to the chair to continue the IB fitting. Pull the piping cord of the wing taut into the corner and pin the cord into the chair. With the OB and wing assembly on the chair, pin the IB along the top seam of the OB. Keeping a straight grain, gently push the tucking fabric into the chair, then pull the tucking fabric out and cut off any excess fabric. A relief cut will enable the IB corner to fold under and lay over the IW. It is best not to fold under an excessive amount of fabric. Once the style line has been determined, a fold of 1" is ideal.

The IB and OB top seam must be sewn before the corners can be closed with the wing assembly.

Once the IB has been pinned along the top seam, remove it, overlock, and sew, stopping short of the corners.

When assembled, return the IB to the chair, pin down the sides of the OW and OB, and sew down this seam. The piping cord can now be sewn in because an accurate corner has been established. Cut the piping cord to length and close the piping.

A relief cut separates the tucking fabric from the top fabric.

Fitting the IB. The fabric fold measures 1" along the back seam and runs to zero at the start of the relief cut.

Ease the IB into the OB seam. Notch the IB and OB, remove, and sew the top seam.

After the top seam has been sewn, return the IB assembly to the chair to close the corners.

Draping the Inside Arm

Keeping a straight grain, drape the block over the IA and pin into place. Make sure that you will have enough fabric to work with in every direction.

Avoid cutting too closely along the SA at the arm front. The OA needs to be sewn to the IA before the arm front is draped.

Draping the IA.

Gently move the fabric into the tucking area, until it is time to release the fabric around the arm curve. Cut as close to the arm curve as possible, without cutting into the SA. To a large degree this is conjecture, as it will not be possible for the fabric to lie perfectly flat since you cannot cut through the SA. You will have to foresee the ideal shape, without actually creating it. Using your hands to coax the fabric toward the seam will help.

Relief cuts are necessary to fit the arm curve. Begin by cutting slowly.

Coax the fabric toward the seam and cut as closely as possible without cutting into the SA.

When draping the IA, refrain from cutting too closely along the OA seam. Pattern changes will be made to the IA before the OA is sewn along this seam.

Once the arm curve has been established along the IW and IA, the two can be assembled. Sew the piping cord along the curve of the IW, and then attach the IA. Once the arm curve has been assembled, close the OW and IA seam.

When the wing and IA has been assembled, return the slipcover back to the chair to fit the OA.

Do not cut too closely along the OA seam. Pattern adjustments will be made before the OA is assembled.

The assembly before the piping has been sewn in. Assemble the arm curve, and then close the vertical seam along the OW and IA.

The finished arm assembly.

Assembly of the IA and OA

For all roll arms, the arm front assembly is never draped as it is upholstered. After smoothing the IA fabric over and under the arm, the length of the IA is dropped .5" below the upholstered line. In this example, the new length of the IA ends at the turquoise line, plus SA. The yellow line illustrates the shape that most upholstered arms would follow, and in this example, the style line must be corrected before the new length can be established. For most fabrics this length will remain unchanged. However, if you are working with a heavier weight fabric, increase the amount of SA from .5" to 1". Because slight shifting does occur during the assembly process, the reserve of extra SA will allow any necessary adjustments, to achieve the best fit. The IA and OA will be sewn at .5", and if an adjustment is necessary, it should be made after the entire slipcover has been assembled. To make changes, open the seam along the OA and IA, release the fabric from the IA, and reassemble.

The OA pattern for a slipcover will follow the outline of the frame. Only the IA and arm front patterns change to accommodate the arm.

How the IA changes for a slipcover. The shape of this arm front curves up and under the chair, and is first shown corrected by the yellow line. The new length of the IA is illustrated by the turquoise line, .5" below the corrected arm front curve. Refer to the club chair slipcover (**PAGE 69**) to view the position of the seam before draping the arm front.

When the IA and OA have been assembled, pin the slipcover into place so that the arm front can be draped.

A close-up view of the seam position.

Draping the Arm Front

The arm front on this slipcover was cut on the straight grain. Because this arm slopes back towards the chair, it will be necessary to cut this arm front on the bias for some fabrics. When the arm front is draped into position, the assembled seam of the IA and OA must be positioned a minimum of .25" and a maximum of .5" below the corner in the arm front, as illustrated by the turquoise arrow in the accompanying photo.

Drape the arm front, and pin into place.

Outline the arm front and indicate notches along the arm front, the OA and the IA.

With an assembled piping cord, sew all three pieces at once, easing and stretching where necessary.

Draping the arm front. The seam of the IA and OA is positioned a minimum of .25" and a maximum of .5" below the corner of the arm front.

Attaching the Deck

Once the arm front has been sewn in, the deck can be fit and sewn. The decks on my slipcovers are always narrow and secured into the upholstery with twist pins, as shown in chapter one. The deck is sewed to the IA at each end, and from there, the tucking fabric of the IA continues into the chair. When dropping a skirt from the deck, proper deck assembly is critical. Similar to the wing assembly, the seams of the IA, the arm front, and the deck must all meet together at one place, and SA must be factored into each pattern. The height of the skirt is decided by the point at which all components can meet. This point will be referred to as "X".

This same method of assembly is used for all skirts that drop from deck height. For decks that have T-shaped cushions and a recessed arm, this assembly point will move to the side of that piece.

A close up of the deck assembly. Notice that the piping cord in the arm front has been cut back so that it does not run through the skirt piping

When draping the IA indicate the X point and then add .5" for the SA. Cut across the IA, the width of the deck. The IA tucking fabric continues into the chair at the end of the deck. Cut the IA, overlock and assemble to the deck. The deck is sewn to the IA the full amount of SA, which is .5" to the red point, after which you will sew to zero to the end of the SA. Sewing to zero allows the deck and the IA seam to lay flat against the upholstery. For more on sewing to zero, refer to the club chair slipcover. The length of the arm front will stop at point X, plus .5" SA which will accommodate the skirt.

Close the arm seam along the IA and deck.

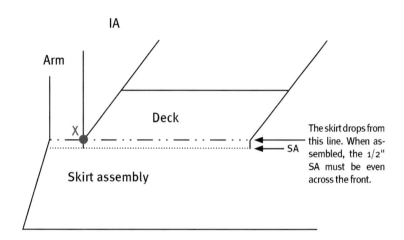

When dropping a skirt from deck height, the red mark highlights the most critical point for skirt assembly. This point determines the height of the skirt because the arm front, IA, and deck seams all meet in one location.

Attaching the Skirt

When attaching a skirt to a slipcover, refrain from fitting the slipcover too tightly around the frame. The bulk of the skirt assembly, especially when working with a heavier weight fabric, can alter the fit considerably. If you are working with a heavier weight fabric, when approaching the piping area change the sewing direction to 1/16" outside of the SA. This will give your slipcover some breathing room, and ensure that zippers will not be drawn together too tightly. In the event that an alteration is necessary, the skirts and the skirt piping will have to be removed to let out the corner seams.

Because this chair did not have a skirt, I lined the skirt of this fabric with flannel to give it more body and weight. To reduce thickness, regular lining was used to back the skirtlets. Otherwise, regular-weight lining is always used to line both the skirts *and* the skirtlets. Contemporary skirts are generally .5" from the floor, and to clear carpet the skirt height should be 1" from the floor. The measurement from point X to the floor is used to calculate the skirt height. In this example, the measurement from point X to the floor is 12", minus .5" to clear the floor, so the finished skirt height is 11.5".

The slipcover has been cut 11.5" from the floor and is ready for the skirt assembly.

The skirt pattern height is 11.5", + .5" SA along the piping, + 1" for the skirt hem, which equals 13".

The lining height is calculated at 13" – .75" which is 12.25". After pressing, the difference in length between the skirt and skirt lining is approximately 3/8".

To assemble the lining and the skirt, sew along the skirt hem at .5". For a slipcover this SA is always pressed upward, ensuring that the seam will not twist with handling. Overlock around the remaining three sides of the skirt

Point X is used to determine the skirt height and this measurement is used to cut around the body of the slipcover before the skirt is sewn in. At the front of the chair, add .5" SA below point X, and measure the distance to the floor. From the floor up, transfer this measurement around the body of the slipcover.

After this seam line has been cut and overlocked, the piping cord is sewn to the slipcover.

Once the piping has been sewn to the body, the skirts can be sewn to the slipcover.

The skirt length is measured from corner to corner, plus a minimum fold of 4" at each end.

The skirtlets are sewn in after the skirts have been sewn to the body. On average, the skirlets are cut 7" wide.

The skirt of a slipcover must cover an upholstered skirt. If a slipcover skirt touches the floor as a result, then glides can be hammered into the legs to slightly raise the chair.

The skirt and the skirtlets.

Note the closing assembly: the skirt closes with a hook, and the side skirt has been sewn to hide the skirt SA.

The Skirt

If a skirt height is the same distance from the floor around the entire chair, then the skirt pattern will be cut the same way. Any adjustments in skirt height are made along the top of a skirt. If your skirt height varies, measure the distance from corner to corner, and the height at each end. After these measurements have been calculated, lay the skirt pattern on the table, fold the skirt ends under (typically 4-6"), and cut a straight line across the top of the skirt. Open the pattern, overlock, and assemble.

Using either frame scenario in the diagram, (if you would like a variable skirt height similar to a womans' skirt, which is shorter in the front and longer in the back) then the adjustment in height would be made along the hem. This, however, does not affect how the top of the skirt would be cut in either scenario.

The skirt stiffener shown above, is a traditional stiffener used to line upholstered skirts. This material is not washable, and in the event that you would like to use a skirt stiffener, the skirt *lining* will have to be slit and bound to facilitate removal. Make sure that the slit is cut along the edge of the skirt fold, as the skirt stiffener is easily wrinkled. Skirt stiffeners will have to be ironed flat with steam before insertion. Be sure to place the inside of the curl (as it comes off of a roll) against the frame of your furniture. This will prevent a tendency to curl outward during hot or humid weather.

Chair (Side View)

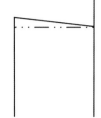

If you choose to drape the seat top along the dotted line, the top of the skirt pattern will be cut straight. If you choose to drape the seat top by following the frame, then the top of the skirt will be cut on an angle. Due to frame limitations, there may be times when this will be the only choice for skirt assembly.

Depending how the seat top is draped, some chair frames will require a varied skirt height.

Chapter Seven
Club Chair

ABOUT THIS PROJECT:
FABRIC BY Waverly
COLLECTION Terra Sole
PATTERN NAME Arabo – Toffee
SKU NO. 649720
VERTICAL REPEAT 1"
HORIZONTAL REPEAT 1"
FABRIC DIRECTION Regular
FABRIC WIDTH 54"
YARDAGE 7.7 yards

A textile supple enough to relax against the IB curve of a club chair will greatly assist you in creating a beautiful slipcover. You may find a fabric that can be draped on the straight grain, but more often than not the IB will have to be cut on the bias. To determine how your fabric will be cut, lay your fabric on the IB of your chair. Depending on the qualities of your fabric and the curve of the IB, seams may have to be moved or extra panels may have to be added to achieve the best fit.

After observing Arabo, I determined that the IB will be cut on the bias. Knowing this, I must be very careful to make an accurate estimate for my block. My yardage estimate for the IB alone is 1.25 yards and includes the 5" of tucking allowance. A pattern such as Arabo can be used on the bias inconspicuously because the pattern is symmetrical. On small areas such as arm fronts, cutting on the bias can be done discretely regardless of the pattern size or symmetry. Using the same method for the IA, I draped Arabo on both the straight grain and on the bias. Once again, I decided to cut the block on the bias. Both directions performed well down the IB seam and across the width of the IA. However, the bias piece wrapped over and under the arm, naturally and without coaxing. For most chairs I fit only one arm and then I cut an opposite. Because working with cross grains can be delicate, I suggest draping each arm individually.

Draping the IB

Mark the bias grain on the block before you begin draping. Smooth the fabric into place from all directions until you get the best fit, and pin into place. The "best fit" is relative to the nature of your fabric and how it relaxes in all directions. If you must move your fabric slightly off the bias grain, then do so.

Along the seam assembly, insert pins into the upholstery of the chair. These notches will be transferred along the seam to both the IB and IA to be used as an assembly guide.

Fold your fabric back as shown and cut as close to the seam as possible. If your fabric will not relax, you will have to move your seam line and/or add extra panels. Your fabric will guide the development of the pattern.

Along the OB, the fabric demonstrates the new pattern outline for the slipcover, where the folds begin. This is approximately .5" higher than the upholstered line. The entire outer seam line will be shaped to smooth into the OA.

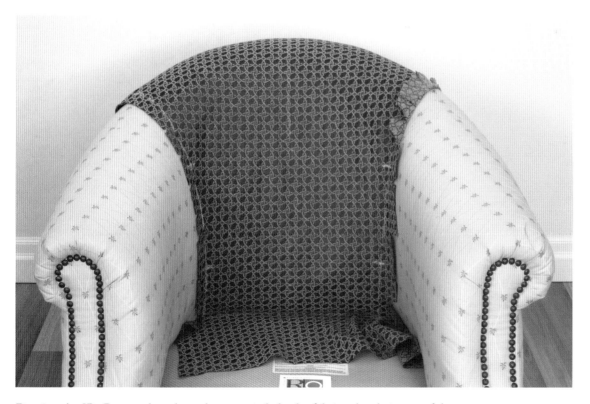

Draping the IB. Cut notches along the seam to help the fabric relax, being careful not to cut into the SA.

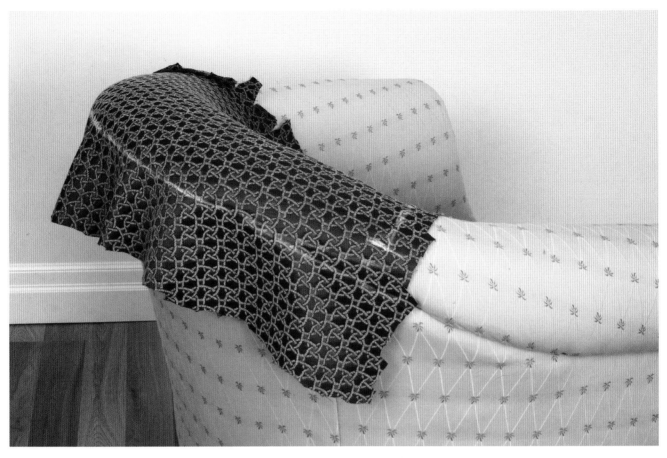

The slipcover pattern is outlined by the folds in the fabric, .5" above the upholstered line.

Draping the IB. The fabric is stretching along the bias, giving way in critical areas. The length of this IB seam needs to be maintained after it has been sewn.

Draping the IA

Drape the IA, and mark down the IB seam, including the notches. Over the roll arm, the new style line is dropped .5" below the upholstered line, plus SA. The pattern can be dropped along the fullest part of the arm and then smoothed towards the back of the chair. In one small area I used a running stitch to gather a small amount of fabric that would not "take" to the chair. This fabric will be eased into the OA.

Before removing the IB and IA patterns, measure the length of the seam on the frame of your furniture. The sewn seam needs to measure the same length, so the fabric will have to be stretched as necessary. The sewn distance from notch to notch must equal the distance from pin to pin on the chair. Remove the patterns, add .5" SA, and assemble. This seam will stop at the deck, where the tucking fabric will be cut straight to the end of the IB length. It will not follow the angle of the seam.

After assembly, replace the IB onto the chair in exactly the same position by placing the chalk marks (notches) over the pins.

When fitting a slipcover on the bias, the tucking fabric will pull on the bias grain, contributing to a better fit.

Press the seams open for a trial fit before topstitching. If you find it necessary to use seam tape, it should be on the bias. I used a very fine invisible nylon thread (.004) to topstitch my Arabo fabric. Regardless of the type of thread you use, the thread tension should be adjusted so that the thread is relaxed and "gives" along the seam. Make adjustments to the thread tension on your machine as necessary.

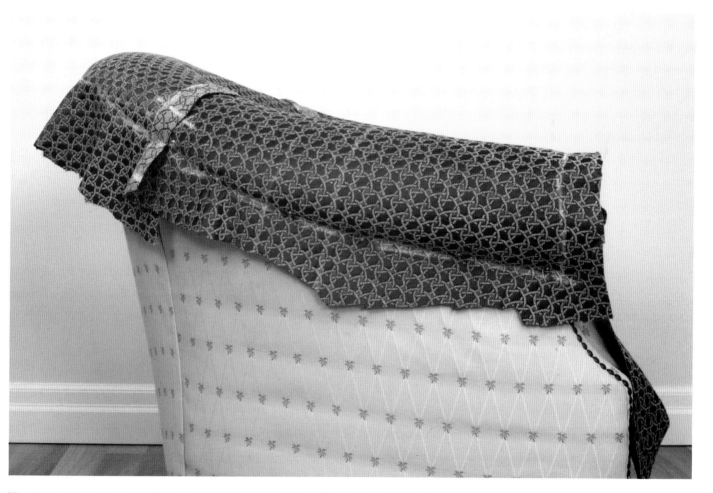

The IA has been dropped .5" along the fullest part of the roll arm. Smooth this line into the IB.

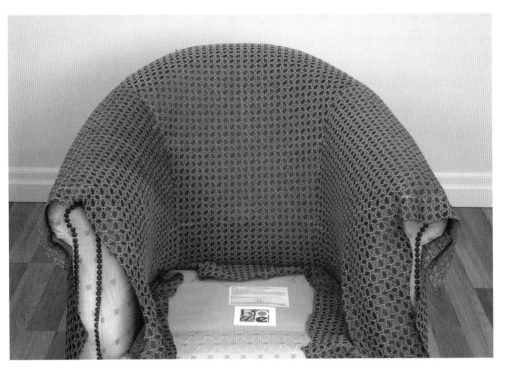

The assembled IB seam stops at the deck.

Draping the OB

The OB and OA blocks have been cut on the straight grain. For the most part, all OB and OA blocks will be cut this way.

Drape the OB, marking the new seam line along the top. Indicate the notches to be used for assembly.

The OB pattern is marked along the new top seam.

Draping the OA

Pin back the OB so that the OA can be draped. The OA pattern is outlined along the frame. As mentioned in the wingback project, only the IA and arm front patterns change for the arm assembly. Mark the assembly notches for the OB and OA.

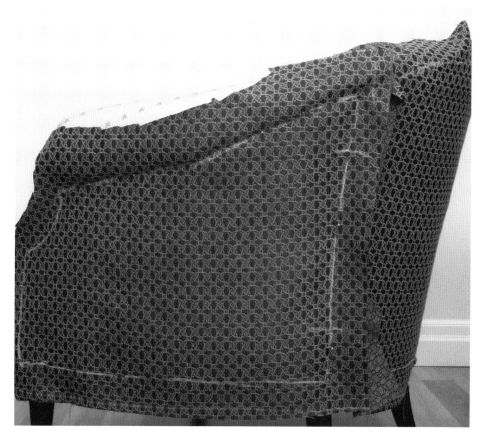

The OA is outlined around the frame. Only the IA pattern and the arm front patterns change for the arm assembly.

When draping the OA let the fabric roll up and under the arm. Cut back any excessive fabric but do not cut an exact SA.

Remove the OA and IB to sew in the zippers. I allocated 1" SA for the zipper.

Allow the OA to roll up under the arm.

Once the zippers have been sewn in, the IB assembly and OB assembly will be returned to the chair for a fitting.

Fitting the IB and OA assembly. The IA length is .5" longer than the upholstered arm. This length is pinned to the OA. The OA is outlined along the frame.

The OB and IB Assembly

Ease the IB into the OB along the top seam; accuracy will be ensured during assembly by indicating notches along both pieces.

As discussed in the wingback chapter, the IA drops .5" at the arm front, plus SA. Because this arm tapers to the back, add .5" only at the fullest parts along the arm and smooth the pattern towards the back of the chair.

Mark along the bottom frame, and add 1.5" for the hem.

Match all notches, and ease fabric when necessary.

Once the OB and IB is assembled, all of the guide pins can be removed

The assembled body is returned to the chair. The underarm seam is placed in position, .5" below the roll arm. The slipcover is ready to be fit for the arm front.

Draping the Arm Front

Because it is not possible for a slipcover to pull into a chair as it is up-holstered in this example, the arm front will be draped as a regular panel. The width and shape of the arm front is usually fashioned along the end of the pleats.

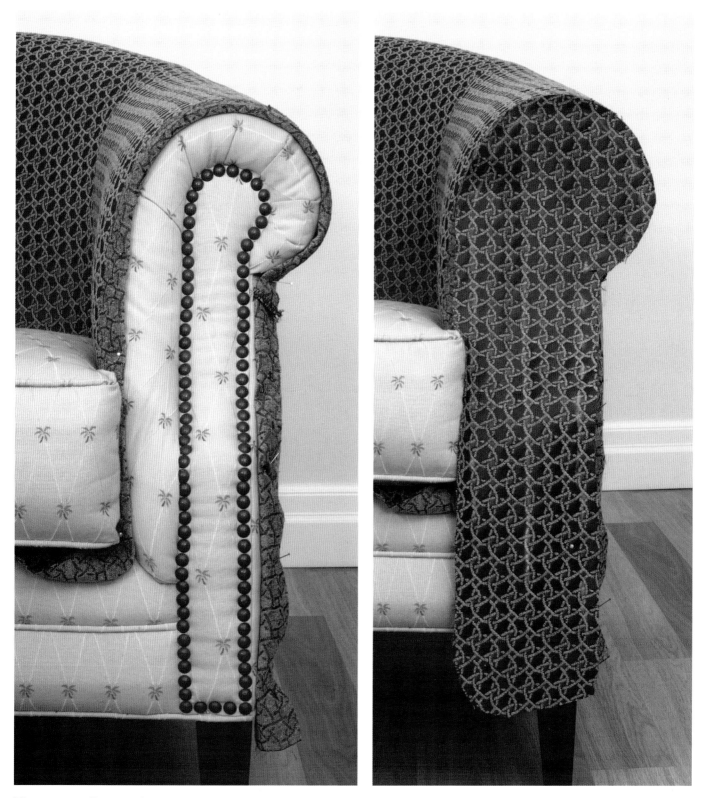

These images illustrate the natural position that the arm front assumes in draping. This seam runs down the side of the seat cushion, but it must be moved forward so that it will run straight down the arm front and be sewn to the nose. Take note of the seam position, which is placed .5" below the upholstered line.

On this chair, the natural position the arm front assumes presents a problem because it runs down the side of the seat cushion. This seam line has to be moved forward so that it can run straight into the nose. This fit process can be a very time consuming play between the arm front and IA, especially when working with cross grains. The uneven upholstery also adds another challenge to the fit process. When completed, the arm front should be balanced, should lay smooth, and the width should be consistent from the top to the bottom of the frame.

The corrected arm front. The IA seam has been moved forward and runs straight down into the nose. Once all objectives have been established, the arm front can be sewn. The sew line for the IA and arm front will stop at the deck.

The finished arm front and nose. The deck is held in place with twist pins.

Draping the Nose

The following photos illustrate the assembly process. All SA must be accounted for.

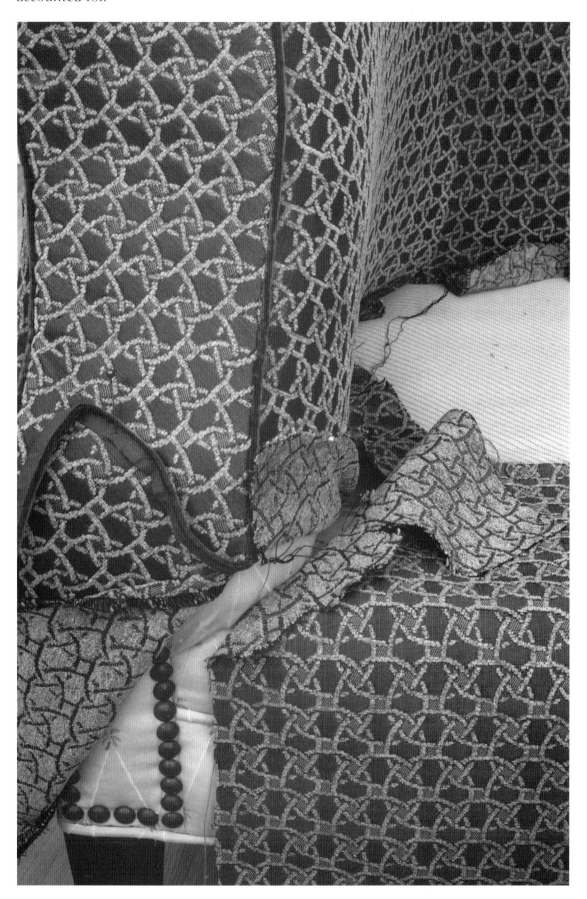

The IA and deck are sewn at .5" to the pink pin, and then to zero at the end of the SA.

Finishing the Hem

A relief cut just short of the frame will allow the hem to separate and fold up around the leg. Mark along the frame and cut the hem 1" below your chalk line. Overlock all raw edges, including the relief cut. Soft Velcro® tape is sewn to the hem and rough Velcro® tape is stapled under the frame. The fabric which folds up to accommodate the leg is sewn in place by hand.

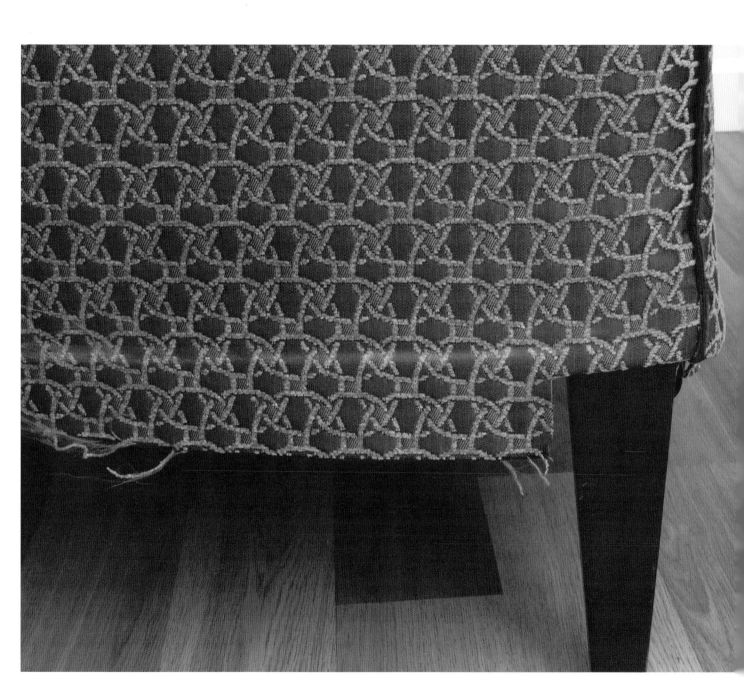

Additional Notes

The finished width across the Arabo seat case was 1" smaller than the original seat case. A combination of tight upholstery, the curve of the IB and the weight of the fabric were all contributing factors.

The original seat insert was built of 4" foam and then wrapped in method C and then A with a 1" poly wrap. This brings the foam and batting measurement to a total of 6". The Arabo seat band was finished at 5", identical to the original.

The IB, IA and arm front were all cut on the bias.

Chapter Eight
Parsons Chair

ABOUT THIS PROJECT:
FABRIC BY Waverly
COLLECTION Williamsburg Language of the Garden
PATTERN NAME Bryan House Trellis – Onyx
SKU NO. 649406
VERTICAL REPEAT 7.375"
HORIZONTAL REPEAT 4.125"
FABRIC DIRECTION Regular
FABRIC WIDTH 54"*
YARDAGE 8 yards for 2 chairs

*The fabric width is 54", but only 50" is embroidered. I used the black selvage to cut the piping along the skirt.

Planning for Repeats

Careful planning is necessary when working with a textile that requires matching. Some prints will fall into the "allover" category and subsequently the yardage estimate and layout will be cut as though the fabric was a solid. Some fabrics will have arrows printed in the selvage which indicate the cutting direction of the print, but most will not. You will have to examine the pattern on your fabric to establish the natural direction of the print. When a fabric requires matching, the chosen motif will be the centering guide for the entire project. The amount of waste will vary, depending on the size of the frame and the repeat on the fabric. Whether you apply a fabric with a large repeat on a small frame, or vice versa, waste is unavoidable.

Many repeats are designed within general specifications, and it will not always be possible to run a print continuously from the top to bottom of a frame. Regardless, the same decisions about pattern placement are made when working with prints that require matching. The following list of questions will assist you with pattern placement.

Q Where would you like to place the motif on the IB?
A The general rule in design is the rule of thirds. This means that your motif will be placed 1/3 from the top of the frame.

Q From the IB, can the pattern run continuously into the seat? If not, where would you like to place the motif on the seat?

Q From the seat can the pattern run continuously into the seat band?

Q From the seat band, if the pattern was to run continuously into the skirt, where is it positioned?

Q If the position on the skirt is not ideal, where would you like to place the motif on the skirt?

Q Which part of your pattern would you like to see in the seat band?

Draping the IB

The side panel detail of this chair would be difficult to conceal with lighter weight fabrics. The weight and texture of Bryan House Trellis does smooth over the side panel detail, but it also requires careful planning in the pleating sequence. Unlike upholstery, where fabrics can be layered and stapled, the same bulk of material cannot always be sewn together. The pleating sequence needs to be pleasing to the eye, it cannot create excess bulk and it must be sewable.

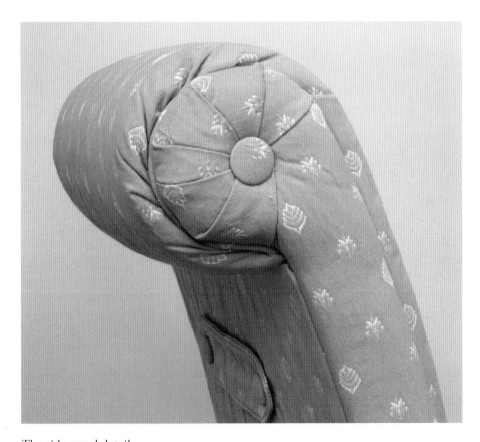

The side panel detail.

When measuring for the IB block, the pleat detail requires extra width. The block needed to drape the IB is 45" long x 34" wide.
Drape the IB block and decide on the pattern placement.

Draping the IB.

When the fabric no longer runs against the chair, a relief cut will release the fabric. Continue with the relief cut until you can pull the side panel straight down. The side length of the IB must reach the skirt, where it will be sewn to the skirt. Avoid cutting into the SA.

Cut away any excess tucking fabric, leaving only the amount which can be tucked into the chair. In this example, my tucking fabric is only 1". If you cannot insert your hand into the frame to gauge the depth, use a ruler.

A relief cut will separate the tucking fabric from the side panel. Cut carefully, so that you don't cut into the SA.

Distance the pleats to reduce bulk for easy sewing.

The last pleat, situated at the green pin, should not extend past the corner of the OB pattern.

The last pleat is typically the largest. If necessary, open any pleat to cut away excess bulk. Cut carefully so that the upholstery on the chair is not exposed. Overlock all the raw edges.

When the pleats are in position, measure the distance along the back, from corner to corner. Assuming that the width of the chair is consistent, this distance will be the finished width of the OB pattern, which is 16" on this chair. The bulk of the pleats should not cluster in the OB corner and the pleats should not extend past that corner.

If the OB frame is not consistent, the OB will have to be draped on the chair. Although the width of the OB pattern has been established, the pattern placement has not. Before the OB can be cut, refer to the next step, draping the OB for instructions. Mark and sew the pleats.

Draping the OB

In the slipcover process, the IB assembly (IB and OB) is attached to a completed arm assembly (IA and OA). Before the OB can be cut, all of the decisions regarding pattern placement have been decided while studying the chair from the front. Once the skirt pattern placement has been decided, then the skirt top can be established. The pattern placement can now be transferred to the bottom of the OB and the OB block can be draped. The pattern will now run continuously from the top of the OB down into the skirt.

In this example, after choosing the position of the pattern on the IB, I chose the pattern placement along the bottom of the skirt. When draping the skirt, ensure that the hem and piping SA is allocated to the skirt block. When the OB and seat pattern placement has been decided, remember to add SA along the break line of the pattern.

Establishing pattern placement on the OB.

After the OB has been cut with proper pattern placement and SA, pin the OB onto the chair. Mark the seam lines along the IB and OB, including the notches.

After establishing the repeat position, the OB can be cut and pinned to the chair. Mark the seam lines and notches along the IB seam.

OB and IB Assembly

Taking the weight of Bryan House fabric into consideration, I cut .5" SA along the seams and then sewed at 3/8".

Sew one side entirely and the other only for several inches stopping where the zipper will start. Sew the zipper into place. I allocated 1" SA for the zipper.

The sides are now assembled, but the top seam from corner to corner will not be sewn until the weight of the skirt has been added. A slipcover on a piece such as a parsons chair does not benefit from tension created around the body to keep the cover taut.

Once the sides have been assembled, the IB assembly will have to be pulled over the chair with the help of food-storage-quality plastic wrap. If your cover appears as though its pleats could be taken in, resist the urge to make changes early on. You can fold and tack pleats over by machine closer to the final assembly. You will need the volume that the pleats create in the curve to facilitate dressing and removal.

Plastic wrap will help with the dressing and removal of tighter fitting covers.

Draping the Seat

After the IB has been assembled, the seat can be draped. Using the established hemline, pin the front skirt into position on the chair. The skirt will be used to establish the pattern placement along the seat front. Before cutting the seat block, verify that the block width will allow movement from side to side, so that the pattern can continue down from the IB. The size of the repeat will determine the amount of play needed.

Pin the front skirt into place, using it as a guide to center the seat.

The front skirt is used to establish the pattern position along the seat front.

Pin along the piping and shape a dart in the corner. For the most part, all upholstered seats that do not feature a separate seat band will wrap under a frame and create a rounded corner. Fitting a rounded corner with a slipcover necessitates a curve in the dart. This will pull the fabric down slightly, just as it does when upholstered, and the pattern will no longer be perfectly level into the corner when upholstered.

Fitting the corner dart.

Cut along the IB to release the tucking fabric. The tucking allowance is 1", identical to the tucking allowance for the IB.

A relief cut separates the tucking fabric from the side panel.

The seat and the side panel will be assembled along the back edge only.

Note the side assembly of the IB and seat in the photos. When assembled to the skirt, the IB is not sewn along the edge of the fold. This technique mimics the look of upholstery. The fabric is sewn and overlocked along the back edge only. When the skirt piping is sewn around the perimeter of the slipcover, fold the fabric into place and sew the piping over the fold.

This is the same method used to assemble the tucking fabric for the IB and seat. A "pocket" is created in the tucking fabric which allows your hand to push the fabric into the frame of the chair.

The fold is sewn across when the piping cord is attached.

A pocket is created. This same method is used for the tucking fabric along the IB.

Additional Notes

When establishing the pattern placement for the skirt, be sure to factor the SA for the hem which is 1", the SA at the top of the skirt which is .5", and the distance from the finished skirt hem to the floor.

For skirt finishing details, refer to the wingback slipcover in chapter six.

Chapter Nine
Contemporary Chair

ABOUT THIS PROJECT:
FABRIC BY Waverly
COLLECTION Pathways
PATTERN NAME Martin Houndstooth
– Honey
SKU NO. 649961
VERTICAL REPEAT 1.375"
HORIZONTAL REPEAT 1.375"
FABRIC DIRECTION Regular
FABRIC WIDTH 56"
YARDAGE 5.25 yards

Chairs with curves always present a set of unique challenges when fitting for a slipcover. Depending on the fabric and the degree of the curve, some components will have to be cut on the bias. For the IB assembly, the pattern will always be cut with .5" SA and then sewn at 3/8" on both the IB and OB components. This SA rule does not apply to the arms because they are typically not overstuffed and do not cause outward pressure on the fabric.

As mentioned in previous chapters, do not rely on the print on an upholstered piece to locate center points. Always measure the frame to determine the center points. This IB is a complete sewn assembly, and may not have been pulled over the frame perfectly on center.

Observations and Decisions

This seat cushion is not removable. I know that I cannot drape a large block of material on the seat and tuck all of the fabric into the sides; to do so would result in a slipcover that would need constant adjustments. Instead, the seat will be cut in three pieces – exactly as it was sewn for the upholstered seat.

There are gathers at the front seat. In draping I will discover if they can be eliminated.

The OA and IA will have the same contour along the top of the arm. Once the OA is draped and cut it can be used to cut the IA outline.

All seams will be topstitched.

I used the middle of the houndstooth motif as my center.

The pattern line for the slipcover has been moved so that the IA will end where access to the side of the chair begins. As the photo illustrates, from the arrow and across the back of the chair to the other side, the upholstered chair is closed. This new pattern line will change the top arm, the OB, the OB ledge, and the gusset patterns. Pattern changes for all components will be made during the draping process.

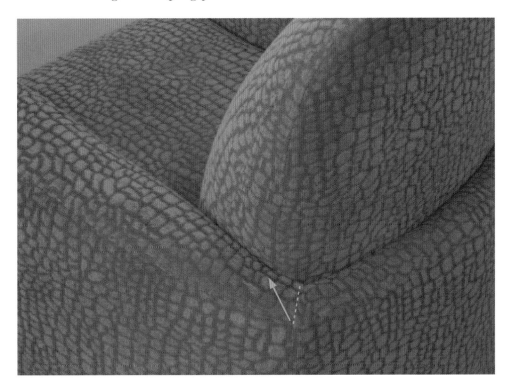

The arrow indicates the new pattern line for the slipcover, which will allow the IA to run directly into the tucking area. The broken line indicates the upholstered seam.

Draping the OA

The bottom frame of this chair slopes toward the back; it is not parallel to the floor. When draping the OA, the pattern must run both parallel and perpendicular to *the floor*, not to the frame. Some fabric weaves, including Martin Houndstooth, will require careful handling so that the pattern is not distorted during the draping process. Smooth the fabric from front to back until it is both perpendicular and parallel to the floor.

Insert a pin into the chair to indicate where the gusset begins.

Insert a few pins along the top arm to be used as assembly guides. These markers will be transferred to all three components: the IA, OA, and top arm.

Chalk along the seam line, to indicate the notches and to outline the bottom frame. You can now cut and overlock all of the IA and OA pieces. Remember to add SA.

Draping the OA.

When cutting the OA and IA the houndstooth pattern must line up both vertically and horizontally in the same position on all pieces. When the top arm is draped, it will allow the pattern to run continuously from the OA over the top arm and into the IA.

When sewing patterns with sharp curves, such as the arm on this chair, sewing a 3/8" SA is preferable to a .5" SA. However, because this fabric is supple and eases well, I was able to sew with a .5" SA.

Along the back of the OA, allocate 1" SA for the zipper.

Draping the Top Arm

From the gusset front, lay a tape on the top arm to determine the grain position. This grain line runs into the shoulder because the arm narrows into the back of the chair. This is the straight grain position that will be used to drape the top arm, and the center of the houndstooth pattern will follow this grain.

Drape the top arm and transfer the assembly notches to the pattern. Because the IA and OA are symmetrical in contour, the notches will be located in the same position on both components. Outline the top arm and remove. Add SA, cut and overlock.

Return the top arm to the chair and check the pattern for accuracy.

Assemble the three pieces together, easing fabric where necessary. Typically, easing will occur along any sharp curve. In this example, the OA and IA are eased into the top arm at the front of the curve. Marking notches while the patterns are on the chair ensures accuracy in assembly. Return the assembled arm to the chair.

The topstitching can be done near the final assembly. This also gives you quick access to the seams should any adjustments be necessary.

The straight grain on the top arm illustrates that the pattern is not symmetrical. The grain is centered at the front but it runs into the back corner.

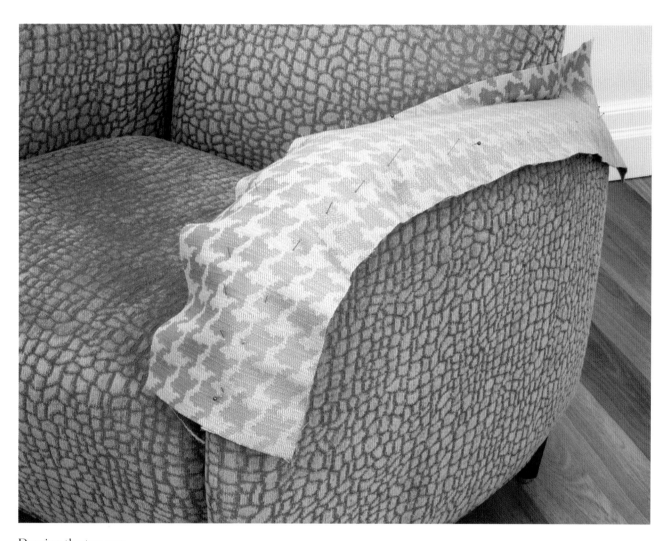

Draping the top arm.

The finished arm assembly.

Draping the IB

Before beginning indicate with a pin the center of the IB between the arms. By eye, bring this line up to the top of the IB and insert a pin into the upholstery to indicate the center.

Feeling for the pins, place the center of the block over the pins.

Keeping the grain straight, ease the fabric into place and pin around the curve. At all times be careful not to distort the pattern. Use a heavyweight thread to baste any areas where the fabric will be eased.

Indicate the point where the gusset will begin. Insert a pin into the upholstery so that this reference point can be used when draping the OB.

On the IB block, make a reference with chalk to indicate where the top arm sits against the IB. The gusset will need to be sewn to the IB at least two inches past this point.

Before the block can be removed from the chair, make sure that all pins that will guide the draping process for other components are inserted into the upholstery.

It is important to indicate the top center of the IB, which will continue down the center back of the frame.

Indicate the end of the sew line when joining the IB and OB. In this example, it is 6" on either side of the center pin. This is where the gusset will start.

Draping the Top OB

Measure the frame of the furniture to find the center points down the length of the entire back. Insert pins into the upholstery along that line.

Drape the OB block.

Mark the top center and the notches where the gusset will begin.

Wrap the fabric towards the back gusset seam so that the new pattern can be outlined. Mark the seam line, and make a reference to show where the OB meets the top of the arm. When sewing the gusset to the OB, this mark indicates where the seam will stop.

IMPORTANT! Before removing the OB, remember to leave a pin in the chair, indicating where the pattern line has moved. You will need this reference point to drape the gusset.

Sew the IB and OB from notch to notch. Return the IB assembly to the chair to drape the gusset.

Ease the fabric into place and pin into the chair, being careful not to distort the pattern. With a heavy weight thread, run a basting stitch whenever fabric will be eased into another component.

Indicate the top center, and 6" on each side, where the gusset begins.

Draping the top OB. The pattern line has been moved to meet with the IA.

Draping the IB Gusset

Following the new pattern line, drape one gusset, keeping the straight grain perpendicular to the floor. Take note of the width of the gusset where it meets the top arm. Using the pins in the upholstery as a reference, measure the width of the other gusset. If the two widths are very different, you will need to drape two separate patterns. If the width is identical, simply cut an opposite, or "mirror."

Indicate with a chalk mark on the gusset where it meets the top of the arm. Remove and add SA.

The tucking fabric—the fabric below the top arm—is cut straight down and is cut back to 6" in length.

Sew in the gussets and return the IB to the chair to verify the fit.

The assembled IB.

Lower OB Assembly

Mark the center of the frame, making sure it is in line with the pattern on the top OB.

Drape the lower OB, ensuring that the pattern is parallel to the floor and that the pattern runs continuously into the OA.

Drape the OB ledge, keeping a straight grain across the length. The centers of all three back pieces should line up vertically. The finished width of the OB ledge is 2.5", but the block width is 6". This is necessary in order to keep the grain straight. Important observations such as this are necessary when measuring and calculating yardage. The new pattern line for the OB ledge will meet the back gusset line.

Where the top OB and OB ledge meet, the upholstery in the chair dips into the frame. Allow the fabric of the OB ledge to lay into this crevice when draping.

Allow 1" for zipper seams and 1.5" for hems.

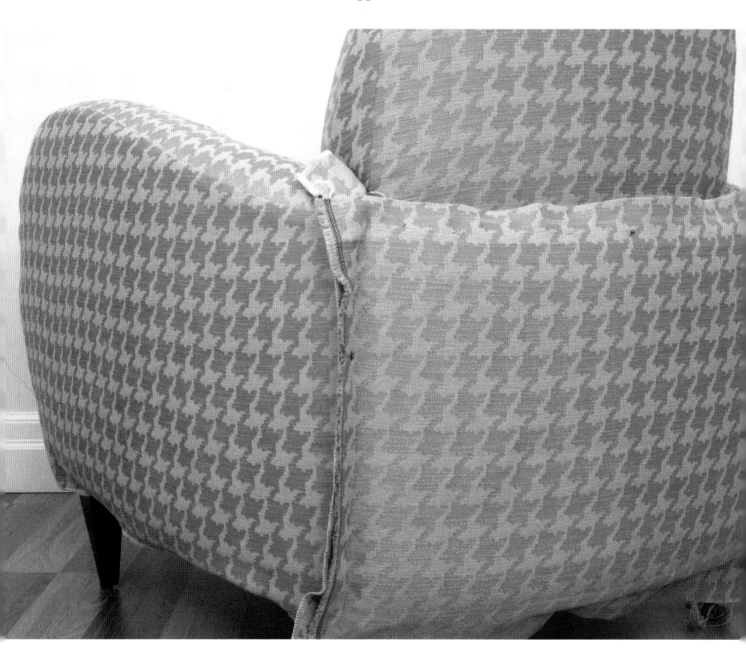

Draping the lower OB. The pattern runs continuously into the OA and vertically through the top OB, the back ledge and the lower OB.

Draping the OB ledge. In order to drape this ledge on a straight grain the block width is cut 6". The finished width of the ledge is 2.5".

Draping the Seat

Measure the frame and mark the center on the nose and the seat. Drape the seat block so that center of the pattern lines up with the IB. Tuck the fabric down the sides of the seat, and outline the seat and the bottom of the frame along the nose. Along the bottom of the frame, where the seat will be sewn to the IA, be careful not to cut off too much SA.

Draping the side panel.

The final seat assembly.

Heavyweight thread was used to gather the fabric on the seat curve. On the side of the seat, insert several pins into the upholstery and transfer these marks onto the seat pattern. These points will be used to drape and assemble the side panels to the seat.

Remove the seat; add SA and overlock.

Place the side panel down into the sides of the seat. The side panel should run down into the chair as far as possible without bunching, and the tucking fabric should lay flat. Make any necessary relief cuts to accommodate structural components inside of the chair. Outline the side panel, and transfer the match points.

Assemble the seat and the two side panels.

On this slipcover, the gathers on Martin Houndstooth appear more prominent than the gathers on the upholstered chair. The texture of Martin Houndstooth is one factor. In upholstery, the fabric is pulled back under tension, but with slipcovers sometimes pockets of air can occur. This is especially true in this example, where the seat sides are tucked down along the frame and do not benefit from wrapping under the chair frame.

Final Assembly

Topstitch all pieces in preparation for the assembly. This will flatten all seams and ensure that each component is smoothed out and can be pulled taut before the final assembly. Make alterations as necessary. The gusset length, which I initially cut bck to 6", was cut again to 2" below the top arm. The bulk of tucking fabric from all components in a tightly upholstered chair prompted the adjustment. Remember that it is important to keep all excessive pressure off of the upholstery. For a lighter weight fabric, the tucking fabric would have probably been left longer.

Close one outside seam and sew a zipper into the other side.
Take note of the assembled top OB and OB ledge. The SA has been topstitched towards the back.
The assembled seam of the IA and top arm stops at the back gusset line, where the IA tucks down into the side of the chair.
The top arm and the OB ledge are assembled with a .5" seam. The direction of this seam is just shy of the back gusset seam, slightly towards the front.
The gusset, top arm, IA, and IB all meet in the tucking area.

The SA of the top OB and OB ledge has been topstitched toward the back.

The top arm pattern shown with the SA.

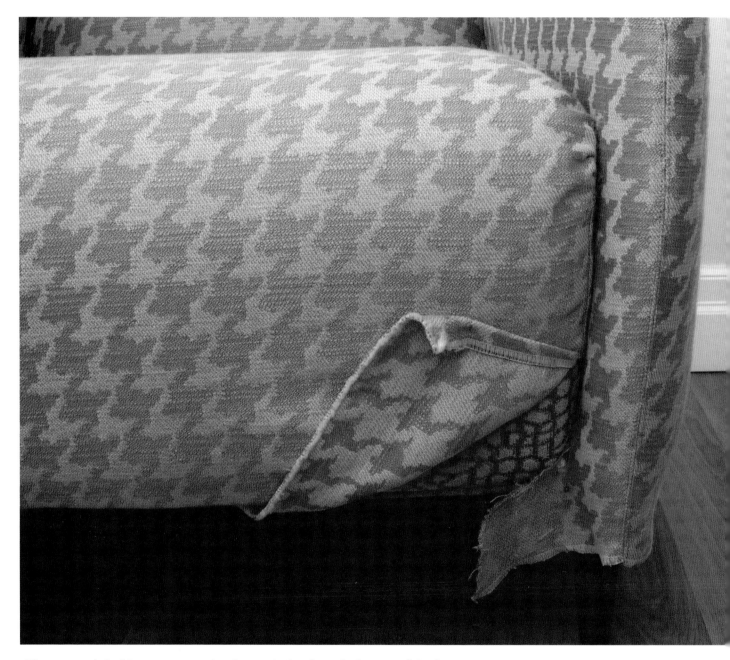

The nose and the IA are sewn together for two inches from the bottom of the frame.

Assembly of the IA and Nose
Finishing the Hem

If your slipcover does not showcase a skirt, the hem of a slipcover will wrap under the frame with Velcro®. Often, you will have very little room around the legs, and your fabric will have to be cut and turned up in this area. Relief cuts are among the most important detail in the assembly of a slipcover, and a proper relief cut will mimic the look of upholstery.

This relief cut is 2" from the bottom of the frame. The cut will separate the fabric from the side panel, so that it can be moved toward the front of the chair to be sewn to the nose. The IA and the seat are sewn together for only 2". The short length of this seam will eliminate seam stress from sitting and movement, and at the same time, allow the slipcover to appear seamless and tailored, and mimic the look of upholstery. The sew line on the IA is indicated by the pin, and SA must be added to the left.

The finished hem.

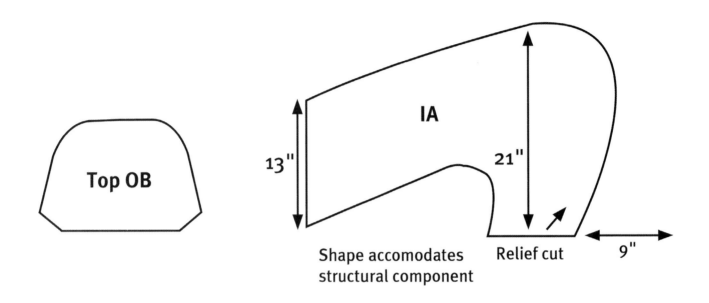

Top OB

IA

13"

21"

9"

Shape accomodates
structural component

Relief cut

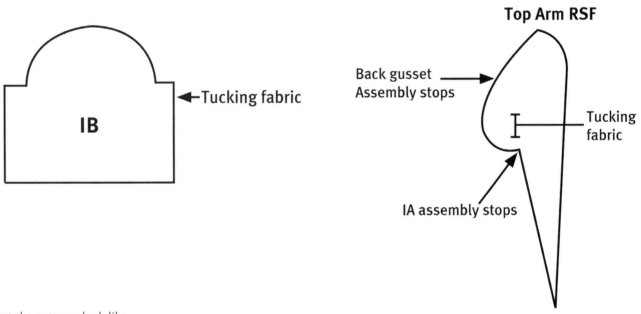

IB

◄— Tucking fabric

Top Arm RSF

Back gusset
Assembly stops ——►

Tucking
fabric

IA assembly stops

What the patterns look like.

About the Author

A graduate of fashion design, Sophia Sevo's textile experience covers garments, furniture and marine goods. Keep in touch with Sophia online at www.tailoredslipcovers.com.

· · · · · · · · · · · · · · · · ·

About Waverly

WAVERLY.

Waverly fabrics are available through Calico Corners, Jo-Ann Fabrics and through local fabric retailers.
The catalogue of Waverly fabrics can be viewed online at www.waverly.com. To find a retailer that sells Waverly fabric, wallpaper and home fashions, please call the Waverly store referral number at 1-800-423-5881.

· · · · · · · · · · · · · · · · ·

About Woeller

The extensive line up of Woeller products includes textiles, lighting, custom made furniture and European leathers. Woeller is available through architects, interior designers and furniture retailers. Showrooms are situated throughout Canada and sales representatives service the international market.
To view a selection of Woeller fabrics and products visit www.woeller.com.
To locate a sales representative, call The Woeller Group at 1-877-963-5537.